NEW DIRECTIONS FROM DON L. LEE

New Directions From
DON L. LEE

Marlene Mosher

Assistant Professor of English
Tuskegee Institute

Foreword by
ARTHUR P. DAVIS
Professor of English
Howard University

An Exposition-University Book

EXPOSITION PRESS   **HICKSVILLE, NEW YORK**

FIRST EDITION

© 1975 by Marlene Mosher

Library of Congress Catalog Card Number: 74-84429

ISBN 0-682-48092-4

Printed in the United States of America

*This book is dedicated to
all of my students at Tuskegee Institute—
past, present, and future—
and to Black educators everywhere.*

Contents

Foreword

Don L. Lee, probably the most influential black revolutionary writer at the present time, is still a young man. He is, therefore, fortunate to have so early in his career a volume devoted to an analysis of his works, particularly a well-planned and scholarly analysis such as that found in Dr. Marlene Mosher's *New Directions from Don L. Lee*.

Avoiding a carping critical approach on the one hand and a too highly adulatory stance on the other, Dr. Mosher has objectively delineated Don Lee's growth as a poet from his first volume of verse down to the last 1973 publication. In addition she has thoroughly examined Lee's critical essays, his social essays, his educational writings and techniques. And—this is of great importance—she has "placed" Don Lee firmly in the background of the sixties and early seventies, pointing out the sources of his literary and social thought. The work, including its excellent bibliography, will be useful, therefore, not only for scholars interested in Don Lee but also for those seeking information on the present-day black literary revolution as a whole.

Because of Don L. Lee's significance as poet, critic, social essayist, and educational writer, *and* because this study has treated so fully and with such insight these aspects of his career, this book is a valuable contribution to the literature of the Black Renaissance.

ARTHUR P. DAVIS
Howard University

Acknowledgments

This book could not have been completed without both the cooperation of several institutions and the aid and encouragement of many people. I am particularly indebted to the National Endowment for the Humanities, for awarding me a post-doctoral research fellowship; to Tuskegee Institute, for granting me a year's leave of absence; and to Howard University, for making its library facilities and classrooms open to me.

I received early encouragement from various people—especially from Professor George J. Worth of Kansas University and Professors Herbert B. Mosher, Youra T. Qualls, and Howard P. Carter, all of Tuskegee Institute.

The critical expertise and advice of the following people had much to do with what is good in this volume: Professor Michael W. Peplow of Lock Haven (Pa.) State College, Professors Arthur P. Davis and Don L. Lee of Howard University, and E. Ethelbert ("Gene") Miller, editor of Howard University's Afro-American Studies journal, *Transition*.

Special acknowledgment is also due to Broadside Press of Detroit, Michigan, for having granted me permission to make frequent quotations from the following works by Don Lee:

Think Black! 3rd (enlarged) ed., © 1969.

Black Pride, © 1968.

Don't Cry, Scream, © 1969.

We Walk the Way of the New World, © 1970.

Directionscore: Selected and New Poems, © 1971.

Dynamite Voices I: Black Poets of the 1960's, © 1971.

From Plan to Planet, Life Studies: The Need for Afrikan Minds and Institutions, © 1973.

Perhaps my greatest indebtedness, however, is to my good friend Waymon Benton, a counselor at Overing House in the Bronx, who repeatedly bolstered my spirits, when they were lowest.

Author's Introduction
to Don L. Lee, Positive Prophet
of a Black Tomorrow

Early in her 1969 introduction to *Don't Cry, Scream,* Don
Lee's third volume of poetry, Gwendolyn Brooks proclaimed:

> At the hub of the new wordway is Don Lee.
> Around a black audience he puts warm healing arms.
> He knows that . . . there . . . [is need for] a violent Change
> —and in the center of a violent Change are the seeds of creation.[1]

A little later she summed up by saying: "Don Lee . . . is a . . .
pioneer and a positive prophet, a prophet not afraid to be positive even though aware of a daily evolving, of his own sober
and firm churning" (p. 13).

Lee's importance, as both a "pioneer" and a "prophet," to
the consciousness of Black America has likewise been recognized
by such disparate leaders as Imamu Baraka, Owusu Sadaukai,
Hoyt W. Fuller, Dudley Randall, Arthur P. Davis, and Stephen
E. Henderson[2]—the last of whom has observed of Lee:

> His poetry is not directed to "white boys and girls" but to black
> people. Nor is he writing for "National Book Awards and Pulit-
> zer prizes," but for his people. . . . His poetry speaks for them
> and to them. . . . His poetry is a weapon for his people at the
> same time that it draws upon them for strength.[3]

Henderson seems almost awed by the responsibility and power
that fall to writers like Lee; accordingly, he asserts:

> Black writers, but especially black poets, can save us, all of
> us. . . . for the [Black Nationalist] Movement is secular now.
> Our poets are now our prophets. They have come to baptize us in
> blackness, to inform us with Soul.[4]

1

It was with these and other similar comments in mind that this author undertook the present assessment of the message and impact of Don L. Lee.

Careful study of Lee and his works indicates that Don Lee does very consciously advance, at all times, "alternatives to Whiteness"; he supports Black culture, a Black aesthetic, a Black value system, and a Black lifestyle. He strives, through his works, to protect Black people from what Henderson has called "the intellectual and spiritual arrogance which masquerades as integration and which has assaulted . . . [Blacks], in one form or another, for nearly four hundred years."[5] To attain this end, Lee calls all "Blackpeople" to him, fills his works and his speech with positive images of Blacks, and attempts to fill his audiences with the wisdom, the confidence, and the courage to become shapers of what Hoyt W. Fuller has called a "Black Tomorrow."[6]

These goals are diametrically opposed to the prevailing aims of White America, which aims Lee sees as being wholly detrimental to Blacks. When America calls "Black people," she calls, according to Lee, in the following manner:

> America calling.
> negroes.
> can you dance?
> play foot/baseball?
> nanny?
> cook?
> needed now. negroes
> who can entertain
> ONLY.
> others not
> wanted.
> (& are considered extremely dangerous).[7]

America is clearly calling Black people only to a position of second-class citizenship, to a self-demeaning position where, as "negroes," Black people would serve as little more than tools of, or entertainers for, Whites. Lee would have Blacks aspire to— and attain—first-class citizenship; he would have them "be an extension of everything beautiful & powerful." Hence, when Lee calls "Blackpeople"—through his speech, through his writing, and through various recordings of him reading his poetry—he calls in the following vein:

> HEY   blackman look like
> you'd be named something
> like . . . . *earth, sun*
> or *mountain.*
> Go head, *universe*
> . . . .
> be it,
> blackman.[8]

Even Lee's use of "combination words" like "Blackman" and "Blackpeople" subtly reinforces two of his main underlying themes (and goals): Black unity and Black power.

Such a positive message as Lee transmits is indeed often an "extremely dangerous" challenge to the status quo of White America. It is likewise a challenge to complacent Blacks. Lee takes very seriously his belief that the function of a Black poet is

> to expose & wipe-out that which is not necessary for our exis-
> tence as a people. *As a people* is the only way we can endure
> and blacknation building must accelerate at top speed. . . . Black-
> poetry is like a razor; it's sharp & will cut deep[; it's] not out to
> wound but to kill the inactive blackmind.[9]

The poetry of Lee makes clear that he has moved through three distinct phases in his career as a Black man/thinker/writer: beginning as a rather quiet accommodationist, Lee passed through an intensely reactionary transitional period before he achieved his present revolutionary status. In his early reactionary works he attempted to point out White evils, to subvert and overthrow—by force, if necessary—a corrupt and decadent White Establishment/Western culture. He soon shifted his emphasis, for the most part, from anti-White/European to pro-Black/Afrikan.[10] From being largely negative and past/present focused, his work became both highly positive and present/future

oriented. This steady growth is reflected in his early volumes
of poetry as well as in his later, and more varied, works.

Even as Lee himself was becoming more confident and
aware, he was attempting to take other Black people along with
him into this growing confidence and awareness. Whatever his
literary vehicle, he continually worked towards the same goal;
his end has ever been the creation of a viable and self-sustaining
Black Nation. Thus, in *Directionscore* (his collected poems) he
attempts to give all Blacks a sense of unity, purpose, and direction, so that they may finally "finish" their "history" on a successful note.[11] His *Dynamite Voices* (a volume of literary criticism)
attempts to outline the role that Black poet-prophets should
play in nationbuilding, and in *From Plan to Planet* (a volume
of social essays) Lee traces the route that a "together" Black
man will follow as he moves to organize other Blacks—first on
the community level, then on a national scale, and finally on
the international scene. Lee's personal lifestyle, his work as a
classroom teacher, and his publishing ventures all support and
complement his efforts as a writer. This totality of dedication on
Lee's part is necessary because,

> You see, *black* for the blackpoet is a way of life. And, his total-
> actions will reflect that blackness & he will be an example for
> his community rather than another contradictor.[12]

Although at age thirty-two Lee is still a relatively young man,
he has already emerged as a usually *sound*, an always *serious*,
and a totally *committed* Black leader, who not only accepts, but
takes pride in, his Black color. He is knowledgeable about Black
culture and history, and, like Addison Gayle, Jr., he is very conscious of "the Black Situation" in the world today. Because his
words and his actions are determined by this consciousness, Lee
has become widely known as a strident young voice advocating
CHANGE. He is, in fact, quite possibly the most important
literary voice speaking to Black people today, for the literary
"father" of the present Black Nationalist Movement, Imamu
Baraka, daily moves more and more into the political arena,

daily becomes more and more dissociated from the "ordinary" Black man. (This declaration about Don Lee's importance is not intended to deny the value of Baraka as a continuing leader in the Black Nationalist Movement; for it is acknowledged that Black "guides" are needed in *all* areas of the Movement. The Black Nationalist Movement can succeed only through the close cooperation of mutually supportive Black people working in all areas—and at all levels.)

Lee functions, in many areas, as a key Black Nation builder. He is a poet whose books are both cheap and widely distributed in Black communities throughout America, where for the past several years they "have sold phenomenally well."[13] In fact, by 1971 Lee had "sold more books of poetry (some 250,000 copies) than probably all of the black poets who came before him combined."[14] He is a respected critic whose literary essays provide nonrestrictive "guidelines" for other young Black writers and whose social essays outline new directions for other committed Black activists. Lee is a challenging lecturer/poetry reader/ speaker, who appears frequently in Black communities, on college campuses, and at educational and political meetings throughout this nation. His work as a publisher helps to make readily available to Black people new ideas that are both positive and demanding. Through his work as a teacher, Lee is developing a highly competent cadre of followers who are both qualified and determined to disseminate Lee's nationbuilding theories throughout Black America and abroad. Lee is indeed both "a positive prophet" and a shaper of "the Black Tomorrow." He delivers a strong—and an ever-maturing—message to Black people, a message that is continually adapting itself to the ever-changing circumstances of Black men in today's world.

NOTES

1. Gwendolyn Brooks, "A Further Pioneer," in Don L. Lee's *Don't Cry, Scream* (Detroit: Broadside Press, 1969), p. 9.
2. Imamu Baraka is a widely published poet, playwright, es-

sayist, and music critic, in addition to being an influential politician and social reformer, whose base of operations is Newark, New Jersey.

Owusu Sadaukai is both the president of Malcolm X University (in Greensboro, North Carolina) and the national chairman of the African Liberation Support Committee.

Hoyt W. Fuller is executive editor of *Black World* magazine, in addition to being an author in his own right.

Dudley Randall is both a widely published poet and the publisher of Broadside Press in Detroit, in addition to being a librarian with the Wayne County (Michigan) Public Library.

Arthur P. Davis has made a lifelong career of college teaching; in addition he is a significant critic and anthologist of Black literature.

Stephen Henderson, an Afro-American Studies professor at Howard University, is also an influential critic of Black Nationalist literature.

3. See Stephen E. Henderson, "'Survival Motion': A Study of the Black Writer and the Black Revolution in America," in Mercer Cook and Stephen E. Henderson's *The Militant Black Writer in Africa and the United States* (Madison: Univ. of Wisconsin Press, 1969), p. 78.

4. *Ibid.*, p. 72.

5. *Ibid.*

6. See Hoyt W. Fuller, "Dedication," *Journey to Africa* (Chicago: Third World Press, 1971).

7. See Don L. Lee, "Introduction" to *Think Black!* 3rd (enlarged) ed. (Detroit: Broadside Press, 1969), p. 6.

8. See Don L. Lee, "Blackman/an unfinished history," in *We Walk the Way of the New World* (Detroit: Broadside Press. 1970), p. 23.

9. See Don L. Lee, "Black Poetics/for the many to come," in *Don't Cry, Scream*, p. 17.

10. Throughout this book *Afrikan* will be the accepted spelling for *African*, and *Black* (and *White*) will be capitalized. These and other spelling "peculiarities" generally conform to Lee's own usage and are germane to Lee's ideological stance.

As Lee himself explains in some detail elsewhere (on page thirteen of his *From Plan to Planet*), the use of *k* in *Afrika* "symbolizes our [Black people's] coming back together again." The capitals on *Black* and *White* reemphasize Lee's belief that "the problem of the twentieth century" really *is*, as W. E. B. DuBois said long ago in *The Souls of Black Folk*, "the problem of the color-line."

11. See especially Lee's "Introduction" to *Directionscore* (pp. 11-25) and pp. 136-148.

12. Don L. Lee, "Black Poetics/for the many to come," p. 16.

13. Stephen Henderson, *Understanding the New Black Poetry: Black Speech and Black Music as Poetic References* (New York, 1973), p. 390.

14. See "Interview: The World of Don L. Lee," *The Black Collegian*, I (Feb.-March, 1971), 24.

CHAPTER I

Re-Act for Action:[1]
The Poetry of Don L. Lee

A careful study of Don Lee's poetry will reveal that Lee has developed fairly steadily throughout his poetic career, in terms both of perfecting his technical skill and of solidifying the ideological content of his verse. Lee's organic, progressive development follows the general "pattern" for revolutionary development that was earlier described by Frantz Fanon in *Wretched of the Earth,*[2] and this steady movement has taken him to the opposite extreme from what was, before he began to write poetry, essentially an inarticulate, accommodationist position on the controversial subject of White racism. In his "early escape/period," Lee secretly wanted and even "tr[ied] to be white."[3] By the time that he was writing his first two volumes of poetry, however, he was already passing through a strongly reactionary— and harshly, violently, elementarily verbal—period. During this second stage of his development, Lee moved to reject all Whiteness—White people, a White value system, the White aesthetic, and what he and other present-day Black Nationalists call a "European frame of reference."[4] In fact, motivated by his strong hatred of Whiteness, Lee moved, during this reactionary phase, to reject the entire Western tradition—even including those "negroes" who still subscribed to what Lee then considered an essentially decadent Western tradition. As a result of Lee's anti-White, anti-Western bias, his first volumes of poetry, *Think Black!* and *Black Pride,*[5] were extremely negative works.

Shifting his focus from "anti-" (White) to "pro-" (Black), Lee soon began to draw from both his own inner strength and the combined strength of other struggling Black poets. Consequently, in his next two volumes of poetry, *Don't Cry, Scream*

9

and *We Walk the Way of the New World*,[6] Lee's voice became progressively "louder, but softer."[7] Rather than violently attack White evil, he chose to accentuate the positive virtues and abilities of Black people—while still hoping to eliminate the lingering negative White influence on his people. Accordingly, his early vociferous condemnation of Whites was largely absent from his next two volumes—although there still were a number of attacks on "negroes" (particularly in *Don't Cry, Scream*). Developing steadily as he wrote these second two volumes, Lee emerged, in *We Walk the Way of the New World*, as what Gwendolyn Brooks has since called "a new Black [man.] . . . a tall-walker. Almost firm."[8] He had become a Black man who could, with quiet confidence, work with other young Black poet-prophets to give positive "identity, purpose, and direction"[9] to Black people. With this very positive goal in mind, Lee gathered together, in 1971, a collection of his poems called *Directionscore: Selected and New Poems*.[10] The appearance of this fifth volume brought Lee full circle; from being an insecure denier of his Black self, Lee had become a mature, confident, and fluent revolutionary spokesman for Black people throughout the United States.

In the beginning, in what I have called his "accommodationist" period, Lee did not publish poetry. Such silence is fairly typical of Blacks who have allowed themselves to be absorbed within the essentially racist Establishment of the United States. The accommodationist who *does* write, however, strives in his writings to give

> proof that he has assimilated the culture of the occupying power. His writings correspond point by point with those of his opposite numbers in the mother country. His inspiration is European. . . .[11]

and his poetry usually rhymes.[12] The so-called Afro-American writer, then, who has been in effect "colonized" within his native land (the United States), writes according to the predominant White aesthetic of the United States. Just as the earlier actual slave, Phillis Wheatley, laboriously imitated the heroic couplets of the leading English poet of her day, Alexander Pope, so a later, and more subtly colonized, poet like Gwendolyn Brooks would consciously set out to imitate the poetics of Ezra Pound and T. S. Eliot, who were the European-American poetic pacesetters during her "apprenticeship" period.[13] But Don Lee himself, as noted above, published no early accommodationist, or "conventional," poetry.

That Lee did, however, experience an "accommodationist" period is revealed in some of the highly autobiographical, "confessional" poems that he wrote later. Hence, in "Understanding but not Forgetting" Lee honestly discusses his "early escape/ period, trying to be white."[14] And again in "The Self-Hatred of Don L. Lee," Lee admits that,

i,
at one time,
loved
my
color—
it
opened sMall
doors of
tokenism
&
acceptance.

In the same poem, however, Lee condemns this former attitude as revealing his "blindness" at that time. That Lee clearly does *not* hold the same accommodationist attitude at the time he writes this poem is indicated in the concluding stanza of the poem, where Lee asserts:

i
began
to love
only a
part of
me—
my inner
self which
is all

```
black—
&
developed a
vehement
hatred of
my light
brown
outer.[15]
```

This change in Lee occurred, he tells us in "Bloodsmiles,"
on "9/15/63 the day I left this society."[16] Again he condemns
his former attitude, seeing it as reflecting his own considerable
"ignorance." Several examples of just how Lee's "ignorance"
affected his early responses to events that touched him appear
in his poetry; for instance, in the ninth of his "Black Sketches,"
Lee states, rather bluntly:

```
in 1959
my mom
was dead at the
age of
35
& nobody thought it unusual;
not even
me.[17]
```

Since Lee was born in 1942, he would have been seventeen
years old at this time; and this rather callous manner of adjust-
ing to his "colonized" status presumably remained with Lee
until he was twenty-one. Then,

```
in 1963
i
became black
& everyone thought it unusual;
even me.[18]
```

With his new-found Blackness came the desire to know more
about that Afrikan culture which had helped to shape him, and
Don Lee began to read voraciously. He

          . . . painfully
        struggl[ed]
        through Du Bois,
        Rogers, Locke,
        Wright & others,

he says: and finally

        my blindness
        was vanquished
        by pitchblack
        paragraphs of
        "us, we, me, *i*"
        awareness.[19]

Increased racial awareness led to Black pride, and a newly proud Don Lee discovered his ability to articulate, in poetry, just exactly what it meant to be a Black man in White America. In 1967 Lee, in a violent, invective-filled burst of creativity, began to flood Broadside Press in Detroit with a steady flow of poetry. As this stream broadened, it became less violent—but even more effective—for, in Frantz Fanon's terms, Don Lee began to replace "muscular action" with "concepts."[20] Lee matured from being, essentially, a cacaphonous voice crying out in anger against the cruelties of White America to become a confident, steady teacher of Black cultural values, a significant voice in the Black Nationalist Movement.

    That Frantz Fanon was in fact one of those anonymous "others" whose works Lee referred to (in "The Self-Hatred of Don L. Lee") as having read became apparent with the appearance of Lee's first book of poetry, *Think Black!* In his remarks on national culture, Fanon had argued that colonized Afrikan intellectuals, whatever their current "nation of dispersal," must first unite, psychologically, with other Blacks throughout the world, by reaffirming both the existence of and the value of an Afrikan culture that predated the advent of the European colonialists. According to Fanon, even the modern Afrikan who has grown up in America should seek to reassert an *Afrikan* culture and to affirm his own hereditary bond with that Afrikan

culture (*Wretched*, p. 215). In this way, he would at once escape the "mind-forged manacles" of a *European* frame of reference and begin to operate from a more positive *Afrikan* frame
of reference. Such a move is of vital importance to Black people
worldwide, for the widespread European (White-biased) frame
of reference is essentially anti-Black in all important aspects;
for instance, there are no positive self-images, no—or few—successful role-models for Blacks operating from within such an
alien frame of reference. Consequently, European cultural values must be discarded by Blacks and an age-old Black (Afrikan)
value system must be revived and refitted to the needs of modern, and widely dispersed, Afrikans.

Don Lee acknowledges his debt to Fanon in the "Introduction" to this first small collection of poems, and here he also
depicts himself as having been "born into slavery in Feb. of
1942" (*Think Black!* p. 6). By seeing himself in this light, Lee
becomes at one with other colonized Black intellectuals throughout the world. His own conscious attempt to reject the European
frame of reference that the American Establishment has foisted
upon him and to establish a more positive (for him, a Black
man) Afrikan frame of reference is reflected in the very title
Think Black! This attempt to establish an Afrikan frame of reference is also apparent from his introductory remarks, where
Lee asserts that "Black art will elevate and enlighten our people
and lead them toward an awareness of self, i.e., their blackness.
It will show them mirrors. Beautiful symbols." To underscore
his own interest in promulgating Black awareness, Lee asserts
that he himself is "Black" foremost; only secondarily is he a
"poet." His true role as a Black artist, Lee argues, is to be a
"culture stabilizer"; that is, he must "[bring] back old values,
and [introduce] new ones" (*Think Black!* p. 6).

The very first poem in this collection, "Back Again, Home,"
mirrors Lee's own earlier rejection of the White value system
by which he had been entrapped. To escape the "insecurity"
and the "ostracism" that are attendant upon Blacks who attempt
to function within the alien culture of White America, the "ex-
executive" in the poem—after having denied and constricted his

Black "self" for years, in an attempt to succeed within the White Establishment—finally "resigns" his important position, reverts to his former "unprogrammed" (and unemployed) way of life, rejoins his former (Black) friends, and comes "home"—"home" to his Blackness. Only by accepting his essential Blackness, his "otherness" from the predominantly White world that surrounds him, can the Black protagonist of this poem relieve his tension and begin to grow into full personhood (*Think Black!* p. 7). And it is this ex-executive's new position at the end of this poem, a position shared by the younger protagonist of "Education" (p. 11), which seems to have been precisely the position of Don Lee when he wrote *Think Black!* Lee, almost surely the prototype for these Black heroes—as he is for the "meditator" in "Understanding but not Forgetting"—is painfully aware that of "positive images as a child" he had "NONE" (*Think Black!* p. 12), that his "negative images as a child [were]—all black" (p. 13), and that the value system of the predominantly White United States is essentially "mind-crippling" for Blacks: judged by White America's standards, "niggers" always emerge as "the 'Culturally Deprived'"; they are repeatedly "proven" to be "inferior/with technical terms and pretty diagrams" (p. 14). It is Lee's job, then, as an aware Black poet, to reverse this trend—to write a poetry that extolls Blackness while denying, even denigrating, White standards and values.

Such a position on the part of the Black artist corresponds with what Fanon had earlier described as the "phase of consciousness which is in the process of being liberated," and the style of such a writer reflects the intellectual struggle that is going on within him: it "is a harsh style, full of images," says Fanon. "It is a vigorous style, alive with rhythms, struck through and through with bursting life; it is full of color, too, bronzed, sunbaked, and violent" (p. 220). And just such is the vigorous, often violent, style of Don Lee in *Think Black!* For example, in "Wake-Up Niggers" Lee depicts the Lone Ranger (here emblematic of both the White American individualistic hero and the entire Western tradition) as being burned at the stake while Tonto, a non-White, finally asserts his own selfhood and flees to safety, rather than placing his self-interest in a secondary position to that of the Lone Ranger and so destroying himself by remaining. Just as the "third-class" Indian finally left the Lone Ranger, so, Lee argues, Blacks ("second-class" citizens in White America) must stop "following" the White man; they must be "hip" like Tonto was (at least this once) and abandon White values (i.e., the Lone Ranger), returning "home" to their own Black selves and adopting a Black value system.

Just as he rejects White social values, so Lee also chooses to operate outside the bounds of the White aesthetic in *Think Black!* Here the drumbeat repetition of "re-act" in Lee's poem "Re-Act for Action" parallels what Fanon earlier called "the poetic tom-tom's rhythms" (p. 226). It also looks forward to Lee's even greater stylistic experimentation in his next two volumes of poetry, *Black Pride* and *Don't Cry, Scream.* In this poem, Lee plays with the words "re-act," "act," and "actions," attempting to incite his Black audience to

> re-act to whi-te actions:
>
> > with real acts of blk/action.
> > BAM   BAM   BAM
>
> . . . .
> re-act
> NOW niggers
> & you won't have to
> act
> false-actions
> at
> your/children's graves (*Think Black!* p. 16).

The immediate urgency of the need for Blacks to react against White oppression is reflected in the short lines, the abbreviations, the staccato rhythm, the use of the slash (/), the capitalization of "BAM BAM BAM" and "NOW." A similar sense of the need for urgent reaction against

> . . . society—white anglo-saxon,
> > standard setting,
> > example setting,

appears in " 'They Are Not Ready,' " as a Black man, having "PREPARE[D] MYSELF," asserts that he will "continue/ to fight dirty [against White America]" (*Think Black!* pp. 23-24).

The inability of Blacks to assimilate successfully into the "Mainstream of [American] Society" (see Lee's poem by that name, p. 21) is one of the main recurring themes in *Think Black!* Blacks should acknowledge this inability, asserts Lee, and, instead of striving to do the impossible (successfully assimilate into an alien culture while retaining some positive sense of self-hood), they should reorient themselves, "THINK BLACK" (see "Awareness," p. 24), and adopt both a Black value system and a Black aesthetic. Lee himself has done this; thus, he uses mostly cacaphonous free verse and Black "ghettoese" in this volume, abandoning standardized verse patterns and language. This action is completely in accord with what both Fanon (in *Wretched*) and Imamu Amiri Baraka (writing in 1966, as LeRoi Jones) had earlier asserted was absolutely essential for a Black writer functioning in a "colonized" situation: he has dissociated himself from the mainstream of White American literature, by asserting his Blackness first and his status as a poet second; and he has assumed his responsibility as being a positive-image maker for his fellow Black people.[21]

Think Black! is, however, as pointed out earlier, more a volume of "reaction" than a volume of "action"; as such it concerns itself more with the destruction of established White values than it does with the construction of new Black values. And the same preoccupation is apparent, in part at least, in Lee's next volume of poetry, *Black Pride*. The latter volume does, however, reflect both some growth toward intellectual positivism on Lee's part and a sharpening of Lee's poetic techniques.

The now-familiar attack on White values recurs again and again in *Black Pride*, but here it has broadened to include attacks on the entire "Western" tradition—on European values *wherever* they are found. Middle-class Blacks ("negroes," as opposed to true Blacks) repeatedly come under violent attack in this volume. They, with their "raped . . . minds" ("The Primitive," p.

24), function as "toms" ("The Wall," p. 26), as spies (for the
White man) in the Black community. Having completely accepted the dominant White value system of America, these
"negroes" need to be "watch[ed, for they are] . . . enemies of
black people." They have had "their minds [blown] literally with
whi/te thoughts & images of western whi/te woman" ("A Poem
for Black Minds," p. 29). They have accepted both the images
and the values of White America and, as a result, these "negroes"
live meaningless lives; they—the "negro" women, in particular—
confine their thoughts to

> . . . hair styles,
>   clothes
>   face care and
>   television
> ("In the Interest of Black Salvation," p. 21).

They are taught, says Lee ironically:

> Instructive things, such as, to talk on the phone
> for hours, without saying something, to view
> TV, listen to radio & sleep at the same time,
> how to wish the dishes washed, how to be the
> best dressed, brokest employee at work . . .
>   ("Pains with a Light Touch," p. 14).

Such people as these are "wasted" people, according to Lee,
and their only "hope" is to

> . . . . see.
> . . . to come back
>   to us.
> ain't you glad you is/black?
>   me too
>   ("A Poem for Black Minds," p. 29).

That it is completely impossible for successful, meaningful
integration of the various races—particularly Whites and Blacks
—to occur in America is a note that Lee strikes again and again
in *Black Pride:*

> first. the color black/naturally
> beautiful canNot be mixed with whi
> teness . . . . must not
>   it's
> mine. ours . . .
>   . . . .
> . . . me. we. living. they existing
> ("A Poem for Black Minds," p. 29).

Blacks are inherently superior to Whites, argues Lee, as he repeatedly turns the tables against the White racist system of America. Hence, Whites are depicted in revolting, degrading (and usually sexual) images: they are

> . . . maggot colored,
> gaunt creatures from europe
> who came here/put on pants, stopped eating
>   with their hands
> stole land, massacred indians,
> hid from the sun, enslaved blacks &
> thought that they were substitutes
> for gods.

They are "faggots," "sissies," "honkies" ("The Death Dance," p. 31), and "stupid muthafuckas" ("The Wall," p. 26). Lee's images here immediately call to mind the "White devil" stereotype that had earlier been popularized in America by the "Black Muslims" (particularly by Malcolm X, whom Lee compares to Christ in "The Black Christ," pp. 22-23). In fact, much of Lee's separatist doctrine, in this second volume, quite closely parallels the tenets advanced by Elijah Muhammad's Chicago-headquartered Nation of Islam.

Blacks, Lee argues, possess all the virtues that correspond to the various vices of the Whites. Hence, the Black youth in Lee's highly autobiographical "The Death Dance" is repeatedly told by his mother, "son you is a man, a black man." As his self-confidence and pride in his Blackness grows, the youth begins

> . . . to dance dangerous steps,
> warrior's steps.

my steps took on a cadence with other blk/
        brothers.

He can already "tapdanc[e] on . . . / [the] balls" of the White
man, and, he warns, when he dances again, "it will be the
/Death Dance" (*Black Pride*, pp. 30-31). Lee's emphasis here
on the violent physical separation of Blacks from White (and
White-minded) oppressors and on political Third-Worldism (as
opposed to the political isolation of Blacks in America from
other Third World peoples) also appears in "Message to a
Black Soldier," where a dying Viet Cong cries out to the Black
soldier who has just shot him: "we are both niggers. . . ." (*Black
Pride*, p. 27). Implicit in this statement is the idea that the
Viet Cong and the Black soldier should unite and together
throw off their White/European oppressors.

Lee completely rejects the mode of "nonviolent resistance" in
Black Pride and either hints (as in "Message to a Black Soldier") or openly states that physical violence is the only ade-
quate/workable response to White oppression. Hence, in "No
More Marching" he points out that the "marchen/& singen" of
the nonviolent resisters have affected nothing; Black protesters
are still

gettin hit &
looken dumb/ &
smilen (*Black Pride*, p. 33).

He foresees "world war 3" as pitting the forces of the

ussr, england, france & u ass
                vs.
third world
30 million niggers . . . (*Black Pride*, p. 34).

This belief in violent physical revolution against the White forces
of oppression was, however, one that Lee would largely abandon in his next volumes of poetry. The time was not ripe, in
the late 1960s, for physical revolution by Blacks in America, as

Don Lee himself soon realized—particularly after carefully considering the deaths of Malcolm X, countless Black Panthers, and even Martin Luther King, Jr.—all of whom were wantonly gunned down by the established powers they were struggling against. Lee would soon turn away from belief in a physical revolution as being the "answer" to the Black man's problems in America and would place his faith, first, in an ideological "revolution." Such an ideological "revolutionary course leads," as Addison Gayle, Jr., has since confirmed in *The Politics of Revolution,* "through the destruction of the images, metaphors, and symbols created by American mirror makers and forced upon Black people."[22]

This "destruction of . . . [White] images" that Gayle refers to is, of course, largely what Lee has been working towards in his poetry from the outset. In *Black Pride* Lee subtly reinforces his contention that White/Western/European values and institutions are crumbling by having his very language "disintegrate" when he is speaking of such institutions (and people). Hence, the term *White* is never capitalized and is always printed in two parts *(whi te)*; similarly, *Western* is fairly consistently *west ern*, and *Catholic* becomes *cat holic*. In a like manner, Black "toms" are consistently referred to as "negroes" (uncapitalized). That Lee is consciously manipulating his language to reflect, to reinforce his ideas is clear, for he becomes more consistently "irregular" with respect to capitalization, punctuation, and "standard" speech patterns in his next volume of poetry.

There are more "positive" (Black) images in *Black Pride* than there were in *Think Black!* and in this respect Lee comes closer in *Black Pride* to achieving his goal of being a "culture stabilizer" (see "Introduction," *Think Black!* p. 6) than he did in his earlier volume. Such Black heroes as Malcolm X and Langston Hughes—both of whom "told the truth" about the Black experience in America—are extolled by Lee (the former in "The Black Christ," pp. 22-23; the latter in "Only a Few Left," p. 17), and the many Black men and women who appear on "the wall" in Chicago are also meant to serve as positive role-models for readers of Lee's poetry. Hence:

> black artists paint,
>   du bois/ garvey/ gwen brooks
>   stokely/ rap/ james brown
>   trane/ miracles/ ray charles
>   baldwin/ killens/ muhammad ali
>   alcindor/ blackness/ revolution
> our heroes, we pick them, for the wall
> the mighty black wall/ about our business, blackness
>   can you dig?
>   ("The Wall," p. 27).

Although *Black Pride* does contain a considerable number of
reactionary (and, consequently, primarily "negative") poems,
it also contains several works which are far more "positive" than
"negative." Lee is, however, still struggling consciously "to be
as near as possible to the people." He is not yet unconsciously
at one with them—hence, the "distress and difficulty . . . and
disgust"[23] that are evident throughout *Black Pride*.

Don Lee's stance as a poet seems to become somewhat solid-
ified after *Black Pride*, for his next volume, *Don't Cry, Scream*,
differs significantly from the earlier two volumes. In his earlier,
heavily reactionary (and highly autobiographical) volumes, he
was, in fact, often crying out against his White oppressors; in
effect, he was begging them—and their "negro" imitators—to see
their "sickness" and to change—hence, the large number of "negative" poems in those volumes. Rather typical of these earlier
volumes is Lee's concluding query in "Understanding but not
Forgetting," where he, pondering "About the American System,"
wonders:

> . . . will it change
> before it's too late—AND BEFORE I AND OTHERS
> STOP GIVING A [DAMN]
>   (*Think Black!* p. 14).

In his third volume, however, Lee moves into action. The
title, *Don't Cry, Scream*, is significant, for in these poems Lee
asserts himself more positively and makes *demands*, not *re-
quests*. And he directs these new demands almost exclusively at
Blacks and at "Euro-Blacks," ignoring Whites almost completely. Here Lee concerns himself at once with pointing out

and condemning the evils and with praising the many "goods" that are to be found within the Black community—both in America and in Afrika. He challenges his Black readers to act in accordance with these goods and to act to rid themselves of these evils. Lee also very deliberately and carefully replaces the mind-destroying (for Blacks) White aesthetic with his own developing Black aesthetic—the latter of which he outlines in the preface to *Don't Cry, Scream.*

Clearly, several positive forces have been at work on Don Lee since he began writing poetry, and in this third volume two influences seem particularly obvious. The first is the *ujamaa*-based system of Afrikan socialism, which was widely publicized, both in Afrika and in the United States, by Julius K. Nyerere in the 1960s. The second is the doctrine of *Kawaida,* as espoused by Maulana Ron Karenga in his Los Angeles-based United States Organization at approximately the same time.[24]

In *Don't Cry, Scream* Lee, for the first time, chooses his subject matter almost exclusively from the Black world of Afrika and the United States; in fact, in only one short poem— the bullet-riddled, bomb-shattered "communication in whi te" (p. 26)—does he deal exclusively with Whites. However, his poetry in this volume is no less incisive than the earlier poetry was; for as Lee probes and cuts through the various social strata of the Black community, he exposes various "diseased members" within the Black community itself. Middle-class "negroes," Lee's popular butt in the earlier volumes, are several times held up for exposure and ridicule. Black politicians, for example, are attacked in the person of "ed brooke" [sic] who, according to Lee,

> sat at his
> desk
> crying & slashing
> his wrist
> because somebody
> called him
> black
> ("Black Sketches," no. 7, *Don't Cry, Scream,* p. 52).

Such a politician as Brooke is clearly far removed from "the Black Christ," Malcolm X, who was lauded in Lee's second volume. Brooke is even deemed "less" than the nonviolent (but still martyred) Martin Luther King, Jr. (see "Assassination," p. 32). All too often, however, as Lee pointed out earlier in both *Think Black!* and *Black Pride* and as he reiterates in *Don't Cry, Scream,* Black political "leaders" *are* corrupted by the White Establishment through what Lee will later come to call "the European-American Corruptibles": "money, power, sex."[25] Moreover, that such corruptible politicians are not confined solely to the United States's political arena is made uncompromisingly clear by Lee in his "Nigerian Unity/or little niggers killing little niggers" (pp. 43-47), as he exposes various "Euro-Afrikans" on the mother continent (Afrika).

Money, power, and sex can also corrupt potential Black Nationalists, and Don Lee is extremely conscious of this fact. Thus, he repeatedly exposes those Black "hipster" radicals who dress the part of radicals but remain essentially uninvolved in the real struggles of Black people. In "But He Was Cool" Lee effectively "dissects" just such a "super-cool/ultrablack" radical who, for all his "double-natural," his "dashikis [that] were tailor made/. . . his beads," and "his tikis [that] were hand carved," is out of touch with the actual needs of Black people. For all of his surface radicalness, this "hipster" is essentially "ill tel li gent" (or sick, misguided), says Lee (*Don't Cry, Scream* p. 24). Such "super-cool" radicals as these are again attacked by Lee in "Malcolm Spoke/who listened?" for merely

> wear[ing] yr/blackness in
> outer garments
> & blk/slogans fr/the top 10.
> . . . .
> u are playing that
> high-yellow game in blackface
> minus the straighthair.

At once mouthing Black slogans in the daytime and sleeping "with undercover whi/te girls" at night (p. 33), these radicals, like their fellow Black "revolutionist[s]" who "often talked/ of the third world. . . ." while making

... bonds
with the
3rd world
thru
chinese women
    ("The Third World Bond," p. 56),

really contribute nothing positive to the revolutionary cause,
asserts Lee.

    Some Black leaders—in all fields—however, do remain stead-
fastly incorruptible. Among this number in the field of literature
is Gwendolyn Brooks (see "Gwendolyn Brooks," pp. 22-23)
who, like Langston Hughes before her, always tells the truth
about the Black experience. As a truth-teller, she is diametrically
opposed to those Black literary "whores" who accept the White
aesthetic and in doing so contribute to the

mental genocide of blackpeople
while
he/she switches down the
street with
his/her ass wide-open bleeding
whi-te blood
    ("History of the Poet as a Whore," *Don't Cry, Scream,* p. 40).

Lee's violent hatred of these Euro-Black "literary prostitutes,"
clearly reflected in this violent, purposely shocking image, is
reiterated in his appeal to Black writers to "discover" and be
guided by "black aesthetic stars that will damage the whi-
temind," which appeal appears in the final poem in this volume,
"A Message All Blackpeople Can Dig" (p. 63).

    Black musicians, like their fellow artists, Black writers, very
frequently "sell out" to the White Establishment; thus, Lee
laments that he is

real sorry about
the supremes
being dead
    ("blackmusic/a beginning," *Don't Cry, Scream,* p. 49),

as he places the Supremes among that class of "realpeople" who

are "becoming unpeople" (see "Nigerian Unity . . ." p. 46), due
to their having begun

> singin
> rodgers & hart
> & some country & western
>   ("blackmusic/a beginning," p. 49).

On the other hand, one of the musical heroes of the entire
Black Nationalist Movement, John Coltrane, is given his due
by Lee in the title-poem for this volume, "DON'T CRY,
SCREAM," as Lee tries to capture, in the screaming beat of
the poem itself, the characteristic wail of Coltrane's horn.[26]
Coltrane's greatness was that he "gave . . . truth"—and true
images—to Black Americans, says Lee:

> he left man images
> he was a life-style of
> man-makers & annihilator
> of attaché case carriers
>   (*Don't Cry, Scream,* p. 31; p. 28).

Coltrane, with his manly scream of self-assertion, is con-
trasted to Billie Holiday, one of the great ladies of the blues,
by Lee, as he asserts: "(all the blues did was/make me cry),"
whereas Coltrane, by replacing Billie's "illusions of manhood"
with true "man images," made him "ascen[d] into: /scream-
eeeeeeeeeeeeee-ing" (pp. 27-31). Lee's dismissal, here, of the
blues as a nonviable form of Black (mental) protest (one much
akin to nonviolent physical protest) almost parallels that made
by his sister Black Nationalist, Sonia Sanchez, in her "liberation/
poem," when she asserts:

> when i hear billie's soft
> soul/ful/sighs
>   of "am I blue"
>   i say
> no. sweet/billie.
>   no mo.
> . . . .
> no. i'm blk/
>   & ready.

Once again the suggestion that violent actions are a necessary response to White aggression is fairly clear.[27]

The significant role that the Black artist must play in the struggle for Black survival is emphasized again and again by Lee in *Don't Cry, Scream,* as he argues that one important end of "blackpoetry is . . . to negate the negative influences of the mass media" (Introduction, p. 15). It is only as a result of the "anti-self" lessons ("DON'T CRY, SCREAM," p. 29) which are daily perpetrated by the media upon Blacks that Black soldiers can be induced to kill other Third World peoples, argues Lee, for such unconscionable actions are really a part of a world-wide White genocide scheme; hence, in "Hero"

> little willie
> a hero in
> the american tradition,

after being traduced by White imperialists into killing Vietnamese "niggers," was finally killed by them; consequently,

> he
> received his medals
> p
> o
> s
> t
> h
> u
> m
> o
> u
> s
> l
> y
> .
> .
> .

(*Don't Cry, Scream,* p. 39).

Similarly, in "Nigerian Unity . . . " "little niggers" fall right into the schemes of Whites by "killing [other] little niggers"

(p. 43). On a more insidious level, unthinking non-Whites, worldwide, willfully "join the deathbringers club" (bringing death to future Third World peoples) when they subscribe to White-inspired "family-planning" schemes and decide that they "don't want more than two children" (p. 47). Such repeated cries of "genocide" (both "mental" and "physical") were characteristic of the Black nationalistic poetry of the late 1960s, and they served as grim precursors of Sam Yette's searching—and well-documented—exposé of what he considers a worldwide White genocide scheme for doing away with "obsolete" Third World peoples.[28]

The role of the Black poet in halting this worldwide genocide of non-Whites is rather clearly outlined by Lee in *Don't Cry, Scream,* where most of his aesthetic and social ideas seem to fully crystallize for the first time. The Black poet, according to Lee, has a twofold role in the worldwide struggle between what he terms "the unpeople" (White mind-distorters and body-annihilators of non-White peoples) and "the realpeople" (Blacks and other Third World peoples): (1) He must replace the mind-boggling (for Blacks) White aesthetic with a Black aesthetic. He must move away from an "arty" poetry like that advocated by Archibald MacLeish in "Ars Poetica"—a poetry that does not *mean* but merely *bes*—to a poetry whose "most significant factor . . . is the *idea*" (Introduction, p. 15). In fact, Lee argues, "most, if not all, blackpoetry will be *political*"; it "will continue to define what *is* and what *isn't*. Will tell what is *to be* & how to *be* it."[29] Moreover, it will tell these things in "black language or Afro-american language in contrast to standard english, &c." (*Don't Cry, Scream,* p. 15). (2) He must also (as Lee pointed out earlier in *Think Black!*) function as a "culture stabilizer," and Lee does this more successfully than ever before in this third volume of poetry, as he repeatedly points out the pre-colonial qualities of Afrikan life which should serve as models for widely dispersed Afrikans today. Lee has, in fact, been doing both of these things, in his poetry, from the beginning. The real significance of his stated poetic credo in

Don't Cry, Scream is, then, not that it points a new direction for Lee, but that it reveals a new confidence on Lee's part that the course he has been following all along really *is* the "right" course for the modern Black poet to take.

Lee describes, in the final poem in this volume, what he *hopes* will be the future way of life for Black people: "we'll move together," he says,

> hands on weapons & families
> blending into the sun,
> into each/other.
> we'll love,
> we've always loved.
> just be cool & help one/another.
> go ahead
> ("A Message All Blackpeople Can Dig," *Don't Cry, Scream,*
> p. 63).

Lee's emphasis, here, on unity of purpose, on collective work and responsibility, and on mutual faith is quite similar to Karenga's emphasis on those same qualities in his *Kawaida* doctrine. Moreover, such a way of life as this clearly looks back to the traditional *ujamaa*-village lifestyle of pre-colonial Afrika where, according to Nyerere, there were three basic "principles of life": (1) mutual love, or respect, between all people, (2) shared wealth, or goods, and (3) shared work.[30] Both "Black love" (which Lee's sister Black Nationalist Nikki Giovanni refers to in "Nikki-Rosa" as "Black wealth") and the Black woman assume highly significant positions in this third volume of Lee's poetry. Black love is a unifying force among Black people, and the Black woman, unlike the Black man, has seldom "sold out" to the White Establishment, argues Lee again and again in most of the poems towards the end of this volume. As she watches her Black man stumbling, confusedly, through a White-controlled world, the Black woman waits, lovingly, for the "blackman [to return and] take her" ("blackwoman:," p. 54). Such "uncorrupted" (by White values and images) Black women are "the real blackgold," argues Lee

(in "Nigerian Unity . . ." p. 45), and only when their full value
is both known to and asserted by Black men can Blacks resume
their former position of leadership in the world; only then can

> blackpeople
> . . . [move] to return
> this earth into the hands of
> human beings.[31]

By the end of *Don't Cry, Scream,* then, Lee has assumed
the stance of a poet/prophet for his people; he relentlessly
urges them, through his repeated poetic "screams," through
his repetitive, almost incantatory, demands, to CHANGE. For
this reason, if any one poem in the volume might be seen as
a kind of epitome of the entire volume, it would surely be "a
poem to complement other poems." Lee appeals here to all
"niggers"—hippies, liberals, and conservatives alike—to "change
nigger. / . . . change. i say change into a realblack righteous
aim." Each "nigger" *must* "change, into a necessary blackself,"
for only by "chang[ing],/[by] know[ing] the realenemy," can
"niggers" survive in an essentially European-controlled world.
Moreover, Lee asserts, as "nigger[s] change. / . . . be[coming]
the realpeople. / . . . . blackpoems / will change," too (pp.
36-37).

The truth of this last statement is seen in the poetry of Lee
himself. Lee is, indeed, by the time he writes *Don't Cry, Scream,*
what Gwendolyn Brooks calls him in her introduction to that
volume: "a positive prophet, a prophet not afraid to be positive
even though aware of a daily evolving, of his own sober and
firm churning" (p. 13). Seen in terms of Fanon's three "stages"
of revolutionary writing, Lee has achieved the final, or "revolutionary," plateau in *Don't Cry, Scream*: he is intent on "shak[ing]
the people" in this volume; he has "turn[ed] himself into an
awakener of the people; hence comes a fighting literature, a
revolutionary literature, and a national literature."[32]

Lee's new assurance is even more clearly reflected in his
fourth volume of poetry, *We Walk the Way of the New World,*
which differs primarily from his third volume not in *content*

(i.e., ideas) but in *form* (i.e., the way in which the ideas are put together). There are, in fact, essentially no "new" *ideas* in this volume. Lee is still functioning as a poet/prophet who advocates CHANGE. He is still pursuing his own multi-faceted role as establisher, and entrencher, of both a Black aesthetic and an Afrikan frame of reference. He also continues to reassert the contemporary validity/functionality of certain pre-colonial (Afrikan) cultural values. Moreover, the final "goal" towards which Lee aims the poems in this fourth volume is still the making of the earth into a *people*-centered place. And all of these ideas had surfaced earlier in Lee's poetry—at least by the time of *Don't Cry, Scream.* The essential difference between Lee's third and fourth volumes, then, is not one of *kind;* rather, it is a difference of *degree. Don't Cry, Scream* might almost be seen as a kind of *improvisational* volume, in which Lee presents his various themes (many by now quite familiar)—and even plays variations on these themes—in a somewhat haphazard manner. That is, there is little structural unity in *Don't Cry, Scream.* Lee is following no particular "program" in his arrangement of the poems in that third volume.

Just the opposite is true, however, of Lee's fourth volume; here the poems—at least the larger groupings of poems—are very carefully arranged, for Lee has his final goal firmly in mind from the outset. Accordingly, in the introduction Lee briefly discusses the book's tripartite structure: "The new book is in three parts," he says:

> *Black Woman Poems, African Poems,* and *New World Poems.* Each part is a part of the other: Blackwoman is African and Africa is Blackwoman and they both represent the *New World.*

Moreover, Lee asserts that "the whole book is based upon the direction I feel blackman should be traveling (*We Walk the Way,* p. 20). In this last statement lies what seems to be the real key to the tight structural unity of *We Walk the Way of the New World:* for this entire fourth volume may be considered as a kind of symphonic poem (or perhaps "fugue" would be a more appropriate term), in which the introduction functions as a prelude to the three main movements. There are, in fact, a great many similarities between this fourth volume by Don Lee and the much shorter (and much more clearly orchestrated) "Dark Symphony" by Melvin B. Tolson.

In the single poem that appears in the introductory section of *We Walk the Way of the New World,* "Blackman/ an unfinished history," Lee introduces "blackman," who is, essentially, the main character in the ensuing world drama. In this introductory poem, Lee summarizes, in brief, the history of the Black man in the United States. Black men were already losing touch with their Afrikan heritage, argues Lee, even when they (most of them) were still in the South. After they took "the trip north / or up south . . . [and] entered the cities" (p. 20), however, their alienation from their essential Afrikanness became even greater; they became

> . . . a part of the pot that was supposed to melt
>   it did and we burned
> and we burned into something different & unknown
> we acquired a new ethic   a new morality   a new history
> and we lost
> we lost much   we lost that   that was
> we became americans . . .
> . . . .
> our minds wouldn't *function.*
> . . . .
> we took on the language, manners, mores, dress
>   & religion
> of the people with the unusual color
> (*We Walk the Way,* p. 21).

By attempting to assimilate into an alien culture, Black men became essentially "anti-self," argues Lee here (as he has so often before). Worse yet, because Black men accepted the European frame of reference advanced by the dominant Whites, their standards of beauty were affected: no longer was the "natural" Black woman an object for admiration; rather,

> we wished her something else,
> & she became that wish.

she developed into what we wanted,
she not only reflected *her*, but reflected us,
was a mirror of our death-desires
(*We Walk the Way*, pp. 21-22).

Black *man*, then, is the real reason for Black woman's Black-self-denial, argues Lee (a point that he had only *suggested* in *Don't Cry, Scream*). Moreover, this self-denial by both Black men and Black women is the underlying cause of the fragmentary state of the Black community (and, by extension, the cause of the nonexistence of a real, functioning Pan-Afrikan community).

The remainder of this introductory poem outlines the "program" which blackman must follow if he is, indeed, to create a "New World" for future generations: first, he must assert, and take pride in, his own Blackness; second, he must instill in his Black woman and his daughters this same self-pride; third, he must focus his attention, his interest, and his desires within his own Black community, where he must strive to introduce, and to live by, a Black value system; hence, he must

design yr own neighborhoods,   Zoom   it can be,
teach yr own children,   Zoom   Zoom   it can be,
build yr own loop,   Zoom   Zoom   it can be,
feed yr own people.   Zoom   Zoom   it can be,
            . . . .
protect yr own communities, Zoom Zoom it can be;

fourth, he must finally expand his interest, moving from just the local community to include the world scene. If blackman does these things, Lee argues,

. . . world greatness is coming. click click.
            . . . .
Go head, *universe*,
Zoommmmmmmmm. Zooommmmmmmmm
Zoooommmmmmmmmmmmm   click   click.
be it,
blackman
(*We Walk the Way*, pp. 22-23).

And blackman, filled with new confidence, presumably moves

off—charging, zooming toward future greatness. In the next
three parts of this volume (or, movements of the larger symphonic poem), Lee shows his readers just what blackman experiences as he attempts to "walk the way of the new world,"
where he first encounters Black woman, then tries to reassemble
an essentially Afrikan value system, and finally works to create
a new, clean, people-oriented world.

In the first movement, "Blackwoman Poems," Lee presents
a rather complex Black woman who is at once "soft," "hard,"
"warm," and "sure" (p. 25). In the several love poems that
appear in this section, Lee emphasizes the softness, the warmth,
and the beauty of the "natural" Black woman, whose love is
so sure that she remains true even "After her Man had left
her / for the Sixth time that year" (p. 36). These usually young
Black women/lovers are complemented by older Black women,
who are both hard (i.e., "durable," or "tough") and wise—like
"Big Momma" (pp. 31-32). Thus, blackman encounters several
Black women who, like the Black heroines of *Don't Cry, Scream,*
are already on the "right track"; in fact, in "Blackgirl Learning,"
"Blackgirl," who writes (people-concerned) love verse that is
reminiscent of "gwendolyn brooks & margaret walker," asserts
that, although her Black man

> worshiped her,
> he wasn't there.
> . . . he had other things to do:
> learning to walk straight
>   (*We Walk the Way,* p. 35).

Presumably, she already can.

Not all Black women are "positive" role-models, however,
and Lee contrasts his healthy, "natural" Black women with
unnatural, self-denying, middle-class "negro" "sisters in two
hundred dollar wigs & suits" ("Mixed Sketches," p. 33). Similarly, in "On Seeing Diana go Maddddddddd," Lee examines
Diana Ross, a "negro" entertainer who has succumbed to what
Lee sees as the essentially White "personal success syndrome."
Diana does "the monkey" (a dance) "with authority," says Lee

ironically (p. 37); then he goes on to depict how she imitates Whites both by denying her physical self—by wearing false eyelashes and a wig—and by completely dissociating herself from the Black community—by caring for *dogs* more than she does for people and by considering her own "bent ego" above all else. Through her total acceptance of the alien European frame of reference, Diana Ross has, Lee argues, "become the symbol of a new aberration, / . . . . [she has] become one of the real animals of this earth" (p. 38). That Don Lee laments the loss of such previously Black, but now "negro," women as Diana Ross is made clear through his use of the refrain from one of Diana Ross's popular songs; Lee (and, presumably, his world-travelling blackman) would draw such wanderers as Diana Ross back to their Blackness "in the name of love"—for, upon the base of Black love rests the foundation of the developing Black community.

Lee's blackman moves on to Afrika, to better consider just what functional pre-colonial Black values ought to be reintroduced into the modern Black community, in the second (and quite brief) movement of Lee's symphony, "African Poems." Here again, Lee (like both Sékou Touré in Guinea and Julius Nyerere in Tanzania) asserts the importance of rural Afrika's maintaining her essentially communal way of life and not allowing herself to fall victim to Western industrialization. Speaking directly to "Africa" in "Change is Not Always Progress," Lee says:

> don't let them
> steal
> your face.

That is, don't allow your essential (rural) nature to be distorted, thus making you into an industrialized, steel giant who

> arrogantly
> scrape[s]
> the
>
> sky
>   (*We Walk the Way*, p. 45).

This message, if heeded by blackman (whose present habitat is the United States), could have considerable importance for the relatively "undeveloped" states of the United States.[33]

A further attack on the causers of environmental ills like those that are presently afflicting the United States occurs in "A Poem for a Poet." Here Whites, motivated by egotism, hypocrisy, and self-interest, consume great portions of the world's natural resources; and, Lee warns, "the waste from their greed/ will darken your sun and hide your moon,/will dirty your grass and mis-use your water" (p. 43). Life in an *ujamaa*-community would, of course, be far more free of environmental "blight" than industrialized areas are; so, Lee further asserts that:

> you must eat yr/ own food
> and that which is left,
> continue to share in earnest
>   (*We Walk the Way,* p. 44).

Self-interest and egotism do not, however, affect only Whites, and blackman, in his brief Afrikan travels, meets a fellow Black from America, Ted Joans, who seems to be a victim of these same "aberrations." Joans, who considers himself "a worldman./ a man of his world" (in "Knocking Donkey Fleas off a Poet from the Southside of Chi"), wanders through Afrika "looking for a piece" (a "piece of tail," or a homeland, or a sense of identity—or all three?), asserting that "blacks must colonize europe," and making egotistical boasts of "I did, I was, I am." Joans, here an example of a continent-jumping "super-cool" radical (much like those domestic "hipsters" that were attacked so vehemently by Lee in *Don't Cry, Scream*), will only "find" his "piece" (that is, his "peace"), says Lee, somewhat ironically:

> . . . (in the only place he hasn't been)
>
> among the stars,   that star.
> the one that's missing [i.e., his essential
> Blackness].

For all his "hipness," Ted Joans is really too caught up with "the rest of the world" to make a meaningful contribution to Pan-Afrikanism (pp. 46-47). Blackman should beware of him, suggests Lee, for the egotistical Joans seems to be far too much like Diana Ross; that is, he functions from a European—not an Afrikan—frame of reference; he is essentially "unBlack."

Having left the geographical limits of Afrika behind him and, presumably, both accompanied by Black woman and armed with a functional Black value system, blackman, in the final movement of *We Walk the Way of the New World*, moves to create, first within the physical boundaries of the United States, that new people-centered community which Lee directed him towards in "Blackman/an unfinished history" (pp. 20-23). This final section reemphasizes the importance of CHANGE—but only that change which is in the right direction, not change just for the sake of change. The importance of the Black community as a social, cultural force is again emphasized, and in "One Sided Shoot-out" (pp. 52-53), Lee reiterates the idea that revolutionary *words* are useless; only united (i.e., community-wide) revolutionary *actions* will finally prevail over the unpeople and give meaning to Black people's lives.

Although there is a "negative" voice in this final movement (as there has been in each of the others),[34] most of the poems here are extremely "positive." In fact, the two most significant poems in this final section—"For Black People" and the title-poem, "We Walk the Way of the New World"—echo the same movement that blackman has been taking in the course of the entire volume. In each of these poems, however, blackman has been replaced, as hero, by Black men (and Black women and Black children). That is, the entire Black race is depicted, in each of these poems, as moving from a state of inactivity (accommodation within, or acceptance of, a White-controlled [and essentially "unclean"] world), through a period of reaction, or protest against that world, and finally into a period of positive action, of self-assertion.

Consequently, "For Black People" is divided by Lee into three distinct sections: "In the Beginning," "Transition and Middle Passage," and "The End Is the Real World." In "In the

Beginning," Black people are forced into ghettoes within the
United States, and they are effectively kept positive-imageless
by the White Establishment's various stratagems: "catholic
churches," "bars, taverns & houses/of prostitution," and "upward
bound programs." Black women are being forced to prostitute
themselves to Jewish landlords in order to buy groceries, and
Black men couldn't care less—for their minds have been confused with images of White women. Mis-educated "negroes"
(who have been educated by European teachers and textbooks)
are operating completely according to a White value system;
as a result, they know mainly "how to be negroes and homo-
sexuals" (pp. 54-56). This is a blighted, polluted world, and the
condition of Black people here is the condition that blackman
was in at the beginning of Lee's volume; it is also the condition
that Fanon described, earlier, as "the period of unqualified as-
similation" into the alien culture.[35] Moreover, this condition was,
as demonstrated earlier, precisely the "inarticulate" condition
that Don Lee himself was apparently in before he wrote *Think
Black!*

In "Transition and Middle Passage," Black people begin to
react to the situation in which they find themselves. They begin
to reject White values and images and "to believe in themselves"; hence, they replace White heroes with Black ones and
read Black writers instead of White ones. Many "negroes" become Black again, and Blacks move to take control of their own
communities. Acting together, the Black community moves to
drive out (or kill) pimps, dope pushers, and other "undesirables." At this stage, "Amiri Baraka wrote the words to the
blk/national anthem & pharoah sanders composed the music.
tauhid became our war song" (pp. 56-58). This period of reaction, in which the awakening of Black people occurs, corresponds at once to blackman's similar awakening, to Fanon's second phase of revolutionary action (see *Wretched,* p. 222), and
to Lee's own psychological position at the time he wrote *Think
Black!* and *Black Pride.*

In "The End Is the Real World," Black people have begun
acting (positively), not just *reacting* (negatively). They have

chosen to follow Allah (the Muslim Supreme Being) rather than Jesus Christ. They read works that are written in accordance with a Black (not a White) aesthetic, and they themselves operate from an Afrikan (not a European) frame of reference. A socialistic economy based on mutual love and respect prevails, and people share both goods and work responsibility. The world has become a clean, peaceful place for people of all colors (although the "few whi-te communities . . . were closely watched," p. 60). This (rather idyllic) world is the world that blackman is trying to structure at the end of *We Walk the Way of the New World.* It is also the world that Don Lee (having attained Fanon's "revolutionary phase" as a writer) himself has been trying to bring into reality through the revolutionary volumes *Don't Cry, Scream* and *We Walk the Way of the New World.*

The program of action that Lee has been advocating throughout *We Walk the Way of the New World*—in fact, throughout his career as a poet—is, then, quite clearly operative in "For Black People." This program of action just as clearly provides the framework for the title-poem in this volume, "We Walk the Way of the New World," where Black people move from accommodation or inaction ("run[ning] the dangercourse") through reaction(having "[run] the dangercourse") and finally into action in "the New World" (pp. 64-66). Both of these poems, in addition to the final "Move Un-noticed to be Noticed: A Nationhood Poem," have a scope, a sweep, an air of victory about them that is reminiscent of the final (and much briefer) section of Tolson's "Dark Symphony." The tone of these poems in particular, and of the whole "New World Poems" section in general, is one that would best be rendered, musically, in *tempo di marcia.* For *We Walk the Way of the New World* emerges as a "victorious" volume: here Lee presents the message he has been preaching all along, but he preaches it more coherently and effectively than ever before.

This fourth volume of poetry marks, then, the culmination of Lee's poetic career: he early set himself a goal, and he has reached it here by effectively using "the past . . . [in order to open] the future, as an invitation to action and a basis for hope."[36] Not content merely to leave "the sometimes seemingly disjointed fragments of the black experience strewn carelessly about," Lee "makes them wholes, integrating them into some kind of meaning, into a historical and cultural context."[37] With this volume, Lee has become a "revolutionary" Black poet in the fullest sense of that term:

> He is an African in America, knowledgeable of his history and culture, who loves his people and who is determined to fight for their survival as a nation. He is outside of American morality, history, and culture and, in so being, he is one who . . . "walks the way of the new world," and charts a righteous path for Black people who follow him.[38]

Through the program advanced in this fourth volume, Lee has truly become what Hoyt W. Fuller, in the "Dedication" to *Journey to Africa,* calls him: "one of the shapers of the Black Tomorrow."[39]

Apparently fully conscious of his important position as "A Strong New Voice Pointing the Way"[40] to a "New World," Lee collected most of the poems from these first four volumes, added five new poems, and in 1971 came out with *Directionscore: Selected and New Poems,* a volume intended, as its title suggests, to provide positive *direction* for Black people throughout the diaspora. Lee's intent in this volume is praiseworthy: he would direct Black people to a better life by providing them with a kind of poetic score which shows the various roles to be filled by Black world-shapers.

Because Lee's intention in *Directionscore* was to provide *positive* direction, he carefully culled most of the negative poems that had appeared in his first two volumes. Thus, seven poems were deleted from the *Think Black!* section, and another seven were culled from *Black Pride. Don't Cry, Scream* lost only one poem, however; and *We Walk the Way of the New World* was presented intact. Instead of taking the time to reorder these early poems into some new "pattern," Lee merely arranged this fifth volume chronologically—a schema which not only saved him time in assembling the volume but also provided his readers with some key to Lee's own growth and development from 1966 to 1971.

Lee takes no new stance in the few poems that appear for the first time here. "Positives: for Sterling Plumpp" reemphasizes the importance of positive "visions of yr self" (or Black people) and stresses that Black poets must "run the mirror of ugliness into its inventors" (i.e., White people, *Directionscore*, p. 199). A direct attack on hypocritical, brutal Whites appears in "With All Deliberate Speed," and the need for Black unity and cooperation is stressed in both "To Be Quicker" and "Mwilu/or Poem for the Living." Gwendolyn Brooks, who has long been Lee's primary poetess-heroine, is lauded in "An Afterword: for Gwen Brooks."[41]

The title of this fifth volume is, then, a little misleading; although there was some "selection" done in assembling the volume, there are only five "new" works included. And these "new" works do not break new ground. *Directionscore* makes it seem that unless Lee were to significantly alter his socio-politico-aesthetic principles, about all he could do—as a poet— would be to keep writing analogous versions of the same program. And repetition has, all along, been one of Lee's major weaknesses. In fact, the frequent repetitiveness of Lee's poetry (and of Black revolutionary poetry in general) has led critic Arthur P. Davis, a rather conservative professor of Black literature at Howard University, to complain that "too much of this hate poetry is repetitive, mouthing over and over again the same revolutionary slogans and themes."[42] Even Dudley Randall, the more radical editor of Broadside Press, has questioned the value of the endless repetition that one finds in Black revolutionary poetry: "One word or phrase chanted over and over with different voices and different intonations may sound exciting when heard, but is it poetry?"[43]

The charge of repetitiveness in Lee's poetry can easily be substantiated (as this essay makes clear), but at least *some* of Lee's repetitiveness may become more "acceptable" when the reader remembers that: (1) Lee's poetry is, above all else, exhortative, and (2) people can better be moved to virtuous action if they hear reiterated just exactly *what* "virtuous action(s)" they are to perform. But it seems that even Lee himself sensed that he was falling into redundancy by the time he had completed *We Walk the Way of the New World;* hence, after that volume, he turned his attention largely away from the writing of poetry and towards both the criticism of other modern Black poetry and the writing of social essays.

NOTES

1. This is the title of an early poem by Lee that appeared in *Think Black!* 3rd (enlarged) ed. (Detroit: Broadside Press. 1969), p. 16.

2. See Fanon's *The Wretched of the Earth,* trans. Constance Farrington, First Evergreen Black Cat Edition (New York, 1968), pp. 222-223—hereafter referred to as *Wretched.*

3. See his highly autobiographical "Understanding but not Forgetting," in *Think Black!* pp. 12-14; quotation appears on p. 13. Also see "Interview: The World of Don L. Lee," *The Black Collegian,* I (Feb.-March, 1971), 24-27; 29; 33-34.

4. See Johari M. Amini, *An African Frame of Reference* (Chicago: IPE, 1972).

5. *Black Pride* (Detroit: Broadside Press, 1968).

6. *Don't Cry, Scream* (Detroit: Broadside Press, 1969); *We Walk the Way of the New World* (Detroit: Broadside Press, 1970).

7. See Lee's "Introduction: Louder but Softer," *We Walk the Way of the New World,* pp. 11-23.

8. See the preface to Gwendolyn Brooks's *Report from Part One* (Detroit: Broadside Press, 1972), p. 13.

9. For more information on the role of the Black poet, see Lee's essays "Institutions: From Plan to Planet" and "The Black Writer and the Black Community" in *From Plan to Planet, Life Studies: The Need for Afrikan Minds and Institutions* (Detroit: Broadside Press, 1973), pp. 43-48; 95-97.

10. Detroit: Broadside Press, 1971.

11. *Wretched,* p. 222.

12. *Wretched,* p. 226.

13. See *Report from Part One,* p. 173.

14. *Think Black!* p. 13.

15. *Black Pride,* p. 19.

16. *Black Pride,* p. 18 (subtitle to poem).

17. *Don't Cry, Scream,* p. 52.

18. "Black Sketches," no. 11, p. 53.

19. "The Self-Hatred of Don L. Lee," in *Black Pride,* p. 19.

20. *Wretched,* p. 220.

21. For Baraka's discussion of the "proper" role of the Black writer in America (which ideas were surely known to Don Lee at the time he wrote *Think Black!*), see his "Philistinism and the Negro Writer," in *Anger and Beyond: The Negro Writer in the United States,* ed. Herbert Hill (New York: Harper-Row, 1966), pp. 51-61.

22. Chicago: IPE, 1972, p. 7.

23. *Wretched,* p. 223; p. 222.

24. See Julius K. Nyerere, *Ujamaa—Essays on Socialism* (New York, 1968). Also see Imamu Amiri Baraka, "A Black Value System," *Black Scholar,* I (Nov., 1969), 54-60, where Baraka carefully outlines/summarizes Karenga's doctrine of *Kawaida.*

25. *From Plan to Planet,* pp. 74-78. (See above, note 9.)

26. The influence of John Coltrane on Don Lee—and on many other contemporary Black poets—has been examined by several recent Black critics. See, for example, Stephen Henderson, "Introduction: The Forms of Things Unknown," *Understanding the New Black Poetry: Black Speech and Black Music as Poetic References* (New York: 1973), pp. 1-69. (Henderson discusses "Don't Cry, Scream" on pp. 54-55.) Also see Bernard W. Bell, "Contemporary Afro-American Poetry As Folk Art," *Black World,* XXII (March, 1973), 16-26; 74-87.

27. For an excellent discussion of Coltrane's influence on contemporary Black revolutionary music, see Frank Kofsky, *Black Nationalism and the Revolution in Music* (New York: Pathfinder Press, Inc., 1970).

28. See Samuel F. Yette, *The Choice: The Issue of Black Survival in America* (New York: Putnam, 1971).

29. Page 16. These assertions about the essential nature of "valid" Black writing echo, almost point for point, the remarks made earlier by Baraka in "Philistinism and the Negro Writer," pp. 57-58.

30. *Ujamaa,* pp. 107-108.

31. "A Message All Blackpeople Can Dig," p. 64. Lee's Black woman in *Don't Cry, Scream* is clearly quite different from his "negro" woman in *Black Pride.* His emphasis on the "positive" qualities of the Black woman in this volume is in keeping with the overall positive emphasis of this work. Lee's view of the Black woman as a culture transmitter/stabilizer is also quite close to that view advanced later by Imamu Amiri Baraka in "Black Woman," *Black World,* XIX (July, 1970), 7-11.

32. *Wretched,* pp. 222-223.

33. In this connection, see Imari Abubakari Obadele I, "Republic

of New Africa: The Struggle for Land in Mississippi," *Black World,* XXII (Feb., 1973), pp. 66-73.

34. Even that sole "negative" voice—the voice of Sammy Davis, Jr., yet another "negro" entertainer—is stilled by "the realdeath the certaindeath" at the conclusion of "See Sammy Run in the Wrong Direction," pp. 62-63.

35. *Wretched,* p. 222.

36. *Wretched,* p. 232.

37. Paula Giddings, "From a Black Perspective: The Poetry of Don L. Lee," *Amistad 2,* ed. John A. Williams and Charles F. Harris (New York: Random House, 1971), pp. 304-305.

38. Addison Gayle, Jr., *The Politics of Revolution* (Chicago: IPE, 1972), p. 8.

39. See Fuller's "Dedication," *Journey to Africa* (Chicago: Third World Press, 1971).

40. See Dudley Randall's "Dedication" (to Don Lee) in *More to Remember: Poems of Four Decades* (Chicago: Third World Press, 1971), p. 5.

41. This poem had earlier appeared in *To Gwen With Love: An Anthology Dedicated to Gwendolyn Brooks,* eds. Patricia L. Brown, Don L. Lee, and Francis Ward (Chicago: Johnson Pub. Co., 1971), p. 135.

42. "The New Poetry of Black Hate," *CLAJ,* XIII (June, 1970), p. 391.

43. *"Black Books Bulletin* Interviews Dudley Randall," *BBB,* I (Winter, 1972), 23-26; quotation appears on 25.

CHAPTER II

Black on Black:
Don Lee as Literary Critic

Late in 1968, in a short article entitled "Black Poetry: Which Direction?" Don Lee considered the question of whether there existed, at that time, such a thing as a "Black aesthetic." After some consideration, Lee made a dual-edged statement in which he asserted that, while a Black aesthetic did, indeed, already "exist," it was, at that time, still not clearly defined. Further pondering this somewhat vague Black aesthetic, Lee queried: "How does one define it . . . or is it necessary to define it?" Moving on to answer his own question, Lee then said: "I suggest, *at this time*, that we not try." (Emphasis my own.) Lee's reason for advocating a time lapse before trying to "define" a Black aesthetic was that he believed, in 1968, that there did not yet exist "an adequate body of work [from which] to determine such an aesthetic." On the contrary, he argued, "Black literature, as we know it, is relatively new." Only "in the weeks, months, and years to come," when "black critics" have had an opportunity to read and examine "the 'new' black literature," will "they, not white boys . . . determine what the black aesthetic is."[1]

According to Lee, then, the Black aesthetic was, in 1968, still a rather vague theory of "the beautiful"—a theory that needed to be developed by Black critics, but only *after* those Black critics had had an adequate opportunity to read and study a substantial body of "Black" literature. To further clarify his position regarding this much-needed Black aesthetic, Lee attempted to distinguish between earlier Black literature and the Black literature of the 1960s. Most of the earlier Black literature was, Lee argued, directed primarily toward "white audiences." Consequently, it also was customarily written in such a manner

45

as to conform to a "White aesthetic" ("Black Poetry," p. 31). Black literature of the Sixties, however, was largely being written to—and for—a Black audience, and it was from the consideration of this later (Black-directed) writing that a meaningful Black aesthetic would, in time, be developed.

Even as Lee was making this plea for "time," however, he himself was moving towards at least a tentative "definition" of that same Black aesthetic. His early critical investigations took four main forms: (1) a number of book (poetry) reviews that he wrote, from January, 1968, through March, 1969, for *Negro Digest* (now *Black World*); (2) several introductions to volumes of poetry by other Black poets that he wrote during this same time; (3) numerous critical statements about poetry that he made in leading Black journals and periodicals at this time; (4) the critical introductions to his own early volumes of poetry: *Think Black!* (1967), *Don't Cry, Scream* (1969), and *We Walk the Way of the New World* (1970). While none of these critical efforts constituted a "sustained" study of the Black aesthetic, together these reviews, introductions, and articles covered much ground; moreover, they brought Lee into direct contact with quite a substantial body of what he himself considered to be "new" Black literature.

As the Seventies approached, conservative Black critics like Darwin T. Turner were, when confronted with the growing need for a clearly defined Black aesthetic, still saying "Wait!" In an essay entitled "Afro-American Literary Critics," Turner pointed out the folly of attempting to define a Black aesthetic when there was not yet a substantial body of Black literature from which to develop that theory. The brunt of Turner's argument was that a wise critic does not attempt to "devis[e] theory prior to the creation of works." On the contrary, he argued, even

> Aristotle actually did little more than examine works which he and other Greeks admired. He distinguished the elements which these works shared. Then he stipulated that great literature must include such elements. Arnold too deduced his theories from literature already created.

Turner considered that it was somewhat foolhardy for "many new Black critics . . . [to be at once] structuring theories [about Black literature and] . . . calling for writers to create the works which are needed to demonstrate the excellence of the theories."[2]

There were Black critics of a more "revolutionary" bent than Turner, however, and these critics believed that a substantial enough body of "new" Black literature already existed, at the end of the Sixties, to enable concerned Black critics to meaningfully define a Black aesthetic. One of these critics was Hoyt W. Fuller, who saw "the late Fifties and the Sixties" as being "important years for Black writers and writing." At that time, according to Fuller, "much of the bound up creativity that had been languishing since the end of World War II burst forth; and scores of [Black] writers—good, bad and so-so—emerged upon the scene, publishing their poems."[3] In Fuller's opinion, then, the early Seventies were ripe for attempting a clear definition of the still vaguely delineated Black aesthetic.

Fuller's views were shared by both Dudley Randall, the publisher of the ever-growing (and experimenting) Broadside Press, and James A. Emanuel, a Black poet, critic, and anthologist. These two had begun to envision a "Broadside Critics Series," of which Emanuel himself would become the general editor. In fact, Randall and Emanuel had visions of the Seventies becoming known as "the Decade of the Black Critic." Their planned Broadside Critics Series would play a key role in earning this appellation for the Seventies, for it would "attempt to introduce a fairly uniform body of sustained criticism into the tradition of Black poetry."[4]

The challenge of instituting this series was offered to—and accepted by—Don Lee, who began, near the close of the Sixties, to put together what would become the first volume in Broadside's planned critical series. Lee's book, which appeared in 1971 under the title *Dynamite Voices I: Black Poets of the 1960's,* was in large part an amalgam of his earlier reviews, introductions, and short critical articles, but some parts of the volume were wholly "new."

The impact of *Dynamite Voices I* was immediate: Hoyt W.

Fuller heralded it as "inaugurat[ing] . . . a crucial new era in Black Literature." *"Dynamite Voices,"* he declared,

> is a landmark book for two very excellent reasons. . . . First, it is the first of several projected volumes in the Broadside Critics Series. What is promised is a number of books by Black critics dealing with the works of Black writers, providing Black viewpoints and Black validation for Black talent and Black perspective. Second, the book is published by Broadside Press, the Detroit-based house which already is the most important publisher of Black poetry in the world and which, with this volume, sets out to corner a share of the prose market.[5]

Fuller's enthusiasm for the volume was generally echoed by other critics and reviewers.[6]

According to these early reviewers, the real value of *Dynamite Voices I* stemmed from two factors: (1) its being the first number in a sorely needed Black critical series; (2) its inherent value as a volume of literary criticism. While the former of these assertions goes unchallenged—for there *was* a dearth of earlier sustained Black criticism of Black literature[7]—a close examination of Lee's text is needed to assure the truth of the latter.

The title *Dynamite Voices* recalls the reader's mind to Lee's fourth volume of poetry *(We Walk the Way of the New World)*, where, in the dedication, Lee had noted his own indebtedness to certain men whom he called "the dynamiters." These men—Richard Wright, Paul Robeson, and E. Franklin Frazier—were, according to Lee,

> makers of new words/ideas that did more than just walk the page, they jumped at us with unrelenting force that wdn't wait.[8]

In *Dynamite Voices I: Black Poets of the 1960's,* then, one would expect to find writers whose works are also "dynamite"—writers whose "new" words and ideas both challenge Black readers and attempt to move them in new, and positive, directions.

Lee's intention in this slender volume of criticism may be further clarified by considering the nature of dynamite. A violent explosive, dynamite is often used to destroy any edifice that has outlived its usefulness and has become, in fact, a hindrance to further progress. As was pointed out in chapter I, Lee's earlier poetry clearly shows that he himself considered the "European frame of reference," its accompanying White aesthetic, and the entire Western tradition to be hindrances to Black progress. Judging from the title, then, a reader would expect that the goal of the writers examined in *Dynamite Voices I* would be to aid in "blowing up," or destroying, the White American Establishment (or at least its entrenched/established concepts), so that something better (something like Don Lee's own "New World") could be constructed in its stead. Indeed, Lee's volume itself (like his own earlier poetry) seems to be yet another intended "dynamiter"; here Lee challenges—and attempts to destroy—the "established" White aesthetic, even as he works to create a viable Black aesthetic.

Dynamite Voices I is divided into five sections (of extremely *uneven* length), three of which are of greater importance than the others. In section one, which he labels "Explanation," Lee struggles both to tentatively define and to leave "open-ended" (or nonrestricting) the long-wayward Black aesthetic. In "The Poets and Their Poetry" (the second and longest section of the book) he examines specific poems by a number of widely read Black poets of the Sixties. Section three, only two pages long, reemphasizes the "threatening" (to the White Establishment) aspect of these "dynamiters," and section four, also a scant two pages, reasserts the importance of Black literature's being a true reflection of "the Black experience." The final section, "A Selected Bibliography of Afro-American Poetry Published 1960-1970," lists significant practitioners of the "new" Black poetry. It is from the critical examination of works by these (and other) Black poets that Black critics will move, in what Floyd B. Barbour has called "the Black Seventies,"[9] to develop a more complete Black aesthetic.

"Explanation" (the "theory" section of Lee's volume) is itself divided into four subsections. In the opening subsection, called "Insights, Hindsights, Going-ons" [sic], Lee explains that, although the *content* of *Dynamite Voices I* is aesthetic, the pri-

mary *intent* of the book is "political." That is, although here
Lee is

> try[ing] to clear up some of the misinterpretations [of], to show
> contradictions and inconsistencies [in], and above all, to give
> direction to that body of Black poetry which exists (p. 15),

the writing of this volume was essentially a "political" act. This
is true, as Lee clarifies later in *From Plan to Planet*, because
"one [cannot] . . . separate the literary from the ideological." In
fact, according to Lee, "everything in this country is political."[10]

In the second subsection of "Explanation," which Lee calls
"Black Critic," he attempts to outline those qualities that he
considers essential to critics of Black literature. Such critics
must, according to Lee, themselves be Black; this is true because "White critics write for white people; they are *supposed*
to; they owe their allegiance and livelihood to white people."
Although Lee is quite aware that *"Being Black is not enough"*
to qualify one as a Black critic, it "is, at this time, a prerequisite"
(p. 17). Critics of Black literature must also "remain detached"
from those works that they are assessing, for only by being detached can one make "fair" evaluations of literature (p. 16).
Lee is convinced that "the best critics are [successful and pub-
lished] creative writers" (p. 15). This is true, he argues, for
such critics' writing abilities—and their confidence in those writing abilities—cause them (1) to be more understanding of the
qualities of the poetry that they are discussing and (2) to be
less inclined than they otherwise would be to make belittling,
envious, "sour-grapes" critical judgments of other—and perhaps
more successful—Black writers (see pp. 15-17).

The true function of the Black critic is, Lee argues, to "giv[e]
some leadership, some direction" to Black writers (p. 21). To
fulfill this function, the Black critic must first be broadly knowledge[able] of world literature, along with [having] a special
awareness of his own literature." His extensive knowledge of
both past and present literature "can provide reliable criteria
for the new critic to use" (p. 20) in establishing (nonrigid)
"guidelines" for beginning Black poets. Black critics must not

try to develop an "ironclad" definition of Black poetry, for to do so would automatically limit it; rather, they must at once offer nonrestraining guidelines and "encourage the young to continue to seek innovative change and valid standards" (pp. 21-22).

In "Black Writing," the third subsection of "Explanation," Lee outlines what seem to him to be salient features of "Black-writing." These characteristics are as follows:

1. Black writing consciously "reflects the true Black experience."
2. The *style* of Black writing is "indicative of that experience."
3. As a result of these first two essentials, "new forms as well as adaptations of present forms must appear" in Black writing.
4. Black writing "is a functional art."
5. It is also "a collective art."
6. It is "committed to humanism" and, because it is also collective, "it commits the community, not just individuals," to this "humanism."
7. Black writing is not "anecdotal," for such writing is considered by Black writers to be "uncommitting and insignificant."
8. "Blackart . . . is *perishable*."
9. While specific examples of Black writing perish, "the *style* and *spirit* of the creation are maintained and reused to produce new works."
10. "Most [Black writing] . . . is social, is art for *people's* sake. . . . Thus the people reflect the art and the art is the people"; that is, Black writing "expresses our [Black people's] attitudes toward the world."
11. Black writing is an attempt "to raise the level of consciousness" of Black people.
12. It is not "mere 'protest' [or reactionary] writing"; rather, it is a positive attempt "to motivate and move [Black] people" to action (pp. 23-25).

Despite his ability—and willingness—to point out these prominent features of "Blackwriting," Lee does not here attempt "to define the Black aesthetic, a varied and intricate area of concepts." This refusal is based upon his forementioned belief that, "by trying conclusively to define and categorize the Black aesthetic, you automatically limit it by excluding improvement, ad-

vancement and change" (p. 24). A clearcut definition of the
Black aesthetic would, according to Lee, eventually lead Black
poets to the same literary "doldrums" that White poets currently
find themselves in. That is, their writing would become "boring";
it would be "over intellectual, pompous, almost without anything
we can touch, subjective to the point of impenetrability, and
rhetorically flat."[11] Lee's emphasis here on the importance of
innovation in poetry is, incidentally, very similar to Albert Murray's insistence upon experimentation, innovation, and variation
in all art (in his *The Omni-Americans*).[12]

In "Publishing" (the final subsection of section one of *Dynamite Voices I*) Lee reiterates the need for wholly *committed*
Black poets. If the modern Black writer is *really* committed
both to Black "manhood" and to Black "nation-building" (p.
27), he will, Lee argues, stop being "dependent for publication
upon his enemy" (the White publisher); instead, he will have
his works published by Black publishing houses (p. 25). This
shift away from White publishers and into Black publishing
houses is absolutely essential for any would-be "dynamiter," asserts Lee in concluding this first section:

> Unless the Black writer helps Black publishers by making the
> Black medium his first source of publication, he will fall into the
> same destructive trap that has engulfed talented Black musicians.
> And Black pride, as most whites wish and predict, will become
> a thing of the past like that "Blackness" of the Harlem Renais-
> sance and the Negritude Movement (p. 26).

(Incidentally, Lee's own publishing policies have, from the beginning, conformed to the publishing dictum presented here.)

Leaving theory behind, Lee moves on, in section two of
Dynamite Voices I, to consider "The Poets [of the Sixties] and
Their Poetry." In the brief prefatory remarks that open this section, Lee discusses the large debt that recent Black poetry owes
both to Black music and to Black speech. He insists that "in
order to deal with the Black poetry of the Sixties . . . it is absolutely necessary to understand . . . Black music at some level,"
for one of "the major influences on the new Black poets [was]

Black music" (p. 30). As a result of this musical influence, "the language of the new writers semed to move in the direction of actual music" (p. 33). The poets of the Sixties became, in essence, "*word* musician[s]" (p. 36), using in their poems "the language of the street, charged to heighten the sensitivity of the reader."[13]

This musical influence also caused Black poetry to become, at times, very confusing to those who would understand it. Lee himself admits that, "in most of the poetry of the Sixties," there are "forms and styles [which are] sometimes as confusing as some of the new Black music forms" (pp. 34-35). In an attempt to lessen some of the confusion surrounding this poetry, Lee lists a number of what he calls "common characteristics of the Black poetry of the Sixties"; these characteristics are as follows:

polyrhythm—uneven, short and explosive lines
intensity—deep, yet simple; spiritual, yet physical
irony—humor, signifying/the dozens
sarcasm—the new comedy
direction—positive movement, teaching, nationbuilding
concrete subject matter—reflection of a collective and personal life style
musicality—the unique use of vowels and consonants with the developed rap, demanding that the poetry be read out loud.

By learning both to identify and to understand the above-listed "forms," one can, Lee believes, begin both to understand and to "categoriz[e] the Black aesthetic" (p. 35).

Since one "can see these characteristics more clearly if [he looks] . . . at some of the poetry" of the Sixties (p. 35), Lee moves, in the body of this second section, to examine specific works by fourteen Black poets who either started their careers or grew to some prominence during the 1960s. Those poets considered are Conrad Kent Rivers, Mari Evans, Margaret Danner, Eugene Perkins, Ebon (Thomas Dooley), Norman Jordan, Sonia Sanchez, Etheridge Knight, Carolyn Rodgers, Donald L. Graham, Julia Fields, David Henderson, Nikki Giovanni, and Everett Hoagland. Some of the poets—particularly Rivers, Jordan, Knight, Sanchez, Rodgers, and Giovanni—receive fairly lengthy consideration, but others—including Evans, Danner, Ebon, Fields, Perkins, and Hoagland—are dismissed after only a few brief remarks. This second section is, then (as is true of the whole volume), somewhat unevenly arranged. Moreover, Lee's critical comments here are sometimes somewhat erratic, occasionally even confusing and/or contradictory.

Throughout his criticism in this second section, Lee focuses mainly on the *ideas* that appear in the poetry being discussed (i.e., on the *content* of that poetry). His discussion of poetic *form* seems, in the case of most of the poets, to be somewhat incidental. That is, a poem's form seems to merit discussion only when it rather strikingly interferes with—or intensifies—the ideas in that poem. This attitude that the *idea* is by far the most important thing about any poem has been held by Lee for some time; in fact, in his 1969 preface to *Don't Cry, Scream,* Lee asserted:

> The most significant factor about the poems/poetry you will be reading is the *idea*. . . . From the *idea* we move toward development & direction.

Similarly, "Poetic form is synonymous with poetic structure and is [merely] the guide used in developing yr/idea."[14]

As he discusses the (revolutionary) ideas presented by these prominent Black poets of the Sixties, Lee reiterates his belief that those poets (like Norman Jordan, pp. 44-48) who are really committed to the Black revolution write so that their commitment is reflected throughout their poetry. Accordingly, after lauding Sonia Sanchez for writing "poetry [that] will not fail to impress the stagnant mind and will open little holes in the blk/brain with poisonlines" (p. 48), Lee shows how Sanchez's poetry purposely becomes "dangerous" to the White Establishment as it "moves to control the negro's reality, moves to negate the influences of the alien forces" (p. 49). The role that the "mystical, yet hard" Black woman assumes in the struggle is examined as it appears in the poetry of both Mari Evans (p. 40) and Conrad Kent Rivers (p. 38), and poems by several authors are praised for truthfully depicting various segments of "the Black experience."

Although the majority of the poets discussed appear to Lee to be consciously trying to provide both direction to and inspiration for Black people, some of the poets seem not wholly committed to the revolution. Lee seems to believe that this non-totality of commitment is reflected in a poet's *form* as much as, or perhaps even more than, it is in the *content* of his poetry. Thus, he takes some issue with Etheridge Knight's "formality" (p. 51), and he objects more strenuously to Knight's frequent use of both classical allusions and "hard words" that send readers scurrying "to the dictionary" (p. 54). Such "elitist" characteristics as these are regarded by Lee as being somewhat irrelevant to the Black struggle. Moreover, long, involved poems like many of Nikki Giovanni's "longer 'militant' poems" (p. 72) should be avoided, says Lee. The Black poet should concentrate on short, unambiguous poems, for "the writer's screening time is limited; therefore, his task should be levelled toward clarity of thought in short forms."[15]

Lee is even more critical of David Henderson, whose "under-worked, over-hipped, pseudo-intellectual 'i can impress u poems'" are all too often almost wholly dissociated from Black people—both in form and in content, but particularly in the former area. Henderson, Lee concludes, seems, from his poetry, to be "a brother who is about to lose the language of his people." Moreover, although "He speaks of music, . . . [he] doesn't show it in his poetry" (p. 67). And both Black speech and Black music have been deemed by Lee to lie at the heart of Black poetry (see pp. 32-34).

Although most of the specific judgments that Lee makes in this second section appear—judging from the numerous "supportive quotations" that are taken from the poems that he is discussing—to be sound, occasionally an example seems to contradict one of Lee's judgments. And there are several other weaknesses in "The Poets and Their Poetry." Perhaps the single most important "flaw" in this section is Lee's often confusing terminology. His refusal to give specific definitions of many key terms leads to frequent shifts in the meaning of some of the terms. Moreover, in his discussions of specific poets, Lee sometimes contradicts his own introductory ("general") statements about the Black poetry of the Sixties, and at other times his judgments are stated rather ambiguously. An occasional evaluatory remark refers to a part of a poem that is not quoted in Lee's text and, as a result, these judgments are very hard to follow. Finally, on occasion Lee uses a poem as a kind of "launching pad" that allows him to move into social commentary of his own.

Probably one of the clearest instances of Lee's failure to support his assertions about specific poems occurs in his discussion of Sonia Sanchez's poetry. Lee first quotes the following lines from her "221-1424 (San/Francisco/Suicide/number)":

> I'm blk. liven in a
> white/psychotic/neurotic
> schizophrenic/society where
> all honkies have been plannen
> my death since . . .

and

> what kind
> of fool are u? what u? some kind of
> wite/liberal/pacifist/jew?
>   all u
> honkies are alike,

then he coolly asserts that this poem "is a minor disaster," since "the words border on being cliches and the slash marks seem non-functional" (p. 50). While the reader is still questioning this judgment, Lee moves on to contrast "221-1424" with Sanchez's "TCB," a poem in which "Sonia [does] . . . the real work." Here Lee quotes the lines

> wite/mutha/fucka
> wite/mutha/fucka
> wite/mutha/fucka
>   ofay,

gives specific praise to Sanchez's selection of "words like 'devil,' 'pig,' 'cracker,' 'honkey,'" and deems "now. that it's all sed/let's get to work" to be "a masterful conclusion" (p. 51). Yet, it seems to this reader that the second poem actually contains both more clichés and more nonfunctional slash marks than the previous one did.

Most of the confusion that exists in *Dynamite Voices I* stems, as Carolyn Gerald indicated in her early review of the volume, from Lee's lack of precise definitions.[16] One example of this (needless) confusion appears as Lee, probably because of his own preoccupation with the importance of brevity,[17] first praises a short four-line poem by Conrad Kent Rivers: the poem in question ("Watts") "becomes a novel," asserts Lee; "and its 14 well-chosen words spell poetry in its purest form" (p. 38). While the reader is somewhat confused to find that the "purest" poem is really "a novel," he assumes that Lee means that "pure" poems are capable of highly concise communication. This belief is strengthened later when, in speaking of Etheridge Knight, Lee says, "He has the ability to say much in a few words. Each poem becomes a complete story" (p. 52). It seems, then, a "positive" thing for a Black poem of the Sixties to be like either a "novel" or a "story." Consequently, the reader is rather taken aback when, later, Lee is extremely critical of Carolyn Rodgers's "Jesus was crucified or It Must Be Deep" for being "not even a prose poem," for "belong[ing] more in the category of a short story or prose sketch" (p. 57). Being like "a short story" has now become a "negative" quality.

When discussing specific poems, Lee sometimes causes his own early introductory remarks to seem somewhat confused—or at least not wholly true. For example, in discussing the "humorous" quality of Norman Jordan's "The Sacrifice," Lee declares humor to be "an element not often seen in contemporary Black poetry" (p. 45). Yet, he had earlier listed "humor" as being one "of the common characteristics of the Black poetry of the Sixties" (p. 35). Similarly, when speaking of Donald L. Graham's poetry, Lee asserts: "He has a message, but it does not lessen his art" (p. 63); yet, earlier (in his remarks on "Black Writing") Lee considered it almost essential for a Black poet to have a "message [of] . . . joy and beauty, pain and hurt"

(p. 25). And again, although he condemns Nikki Giovanni's "Ugly Honkies, or The Election Game and How to Win It" as being "a street corner rap, not a poem" (p. 73), he had earlier found "the developed rap" to be (an apparently "positive") characteristic of the Black poetry of the Sixties (p. 35).

Sometimes Lee's judgments are simply unclear. For instance, on page 43 he cites a number of pre-1960 poets who, throughout the Sixties, "continued to *deathen* us." While Lee's italicized word seems to be making an extremely negative judgment of these poets, the larger context of this statement seems to be praising these "stronger voices" from the pre-Sixties. And again, on page 74, Lee, speaking of Everett Hoagland, says, "He writes about a Black aesthetic"; then Lee proceeds to give lengthy quotations from Hoagland's *love poems,* in an effort to clarify his own statement. On occasion Lee's own "poetic bent" seems to get in the way of his clarity; for example, in speaking of Norman Jordan's poetry, Lee asserts:

> one of the main responsibilities of the poet is to confront these super-idiots [who rule the world]. Brother Jordan does this in geographically positive pictures and images. His are the true eyes of instant feeling, the bold look of the music giver (pp. 47-48).

After reading this passage, one wishes for a clear example of Jordan's method of "confrontation"—but Lee includes none.

Occasionally Lee's commentary focuses on poems—or on passages from poems—that are not quoted in *Dynamite Voices I.* For example, in discussing Margaret Danner's "And Through the Caribbean Sea," Lee asserts:

> Those references or allusions which are not African are meant to indicate a loss of identity; Louis Quinze Frame, Rococo, etc. (p. 41).

Although Lee's statement seems plausible enough, the reader must go to another source if he wishes to check the accuracy of Lee's judgment. The relatively few lines of Danner's poem that are quoted by Lee contain none of these non-Afrikan images.

While this technique of commenting on absent lines is a little unnerving to the reader, it *may* be Lee's subtle way of encouraging his readers to go out and read more of the Black poetry of the Sixties.

Lee sometimes completely abandons the poem he is discussing and moves far beyond it, to indulge in social criticism of his own. One of the most glaring instances of this occurs on pages 60-61, where Lee moves from a cursory discussion of Donald L. Graham's "the patriot" to dwell at some length on the "bitter, but true . . . history of the treatment of the Black man in America." While what Lee says in his ensuing sociohistorical sketch of the Black man in America is true, his commentary bears no integral relationship to Graham's poem; rather, Lee here digresses into his own personal attack on the corrupt but powerful White Establishment in America.

Perhaps because this second section is really the first extended piece of criticism in which Lee deals with works by a number of Black writers, he often buttresses his own critical judgments (whether they are "negative" or "positive") with statements made by other Black critics. Thus, after criticizing certain poems by Carolyn Rodgers for containing "inconsistencies" and "misuses of language," Lee quotes Dudley Randall's earlier review of Rodgers's *Songs of a Black Bird*—where Randall, too, complained about her "unfamiliar spellings" and "typographical tricks" (pp. 58-59). In a like manner, early in his examination of Etheridge Knight's work, Lee quotes Gwendolyn Brooks's assertion that Knight's poems contain "blackness, inclusive, possessed and given, freed and terrible and beautiful" (p. 52). Then he goes on to "prove" this assertion, before making his own judgments concerning Knight's work. Lee's technique is similar as he approaches David Henderson's poetry: after citing—and "proving"—earlier criticism by Imamu Baraka (see pp. 65-66), Lee makes his own assessment of Henderson's work. Lee's use, here, of evaluations made by other Black critics achieves two ends: (1) it makes Lee's readers aware of other Black critics of Black poetry, and (2) it adds some "authority" to Lee's own judgments of the poetry that he is discussing.

Lee closes the text of *Dynamite Voices I* with two very brief
sections, the first of which he calls "Universality of the Black
Writer/Poet: A Blending of Our Yesterday, Our Today, Our
Tomorrow." In this brief section, Lee discusses the familiar
charge (which is usually made by White critics) that Black
writing of the kind discussed in section two of *Dynamite Voices
I* is not "universal"; that is, "Black writers [like these] . . .
'limit' themselves by constantly writing about their own people"
(p. 76). Lee dismisses this charge of provincialism on the
grounds that the notion of "universality" is merely a tool used
by White racist critics as a means of demeaning any Black writing that challenges the status quo in this largely White-controlled world. Lee's advice to Black poets is that they should
familiarize themselves with both past and present Black writing;
in this way their own writing will become an extension, a development, "of past and present [Black] traditions" (p. 77),
and *all* of "the world's people" will ultimately gain wisdom from
the study of works by this "unique and interesting" Black seg-
ment of humanity (p. 76).

In the short fourth section of his volume ("Concluding the
Beginning"), Lee comes back to the question he had broached
in the first section of *Dynamite Voices I:* just what *is* the
"proper" role of the Black writer in America today? Here Lee
reiterates his belief that Black writers, Black image-makers,
have a vital—and powerful—role in the shaping of a Black tomorrow. This is true because Black "poetry, like Black music,
speaks for our time and our people, realistically reflecting the
pains, injuries, and beauty of our world" (p. 78). Lee, like Mari
Evans, is adamant in insisting that it is only by "Speak[ing] the
truth to the people/Talk[ing] sense to the people" that a Black
poet can finally

> Free them with reason
> Free them with honesty
> Free the people with Love and Courage
>   and Care for their Being.[18]

And freeing his people is what Don Lee, critic, like Don Lee,
poet, "is all about" (p. 79).

The final section of *Dynamite Voices I* is "A Selected Bibliography of Afro-American Poetry Published 1960-1970." The purpose of this bibliography is to make Lee's readers aware of the broad range of Black poetry that was published during the decade of the Sixties—both in the United States and abroad. This bibliography is, as Carolyn Gerald has pointed out elsewhere, both "practical and informative." Considerable effort on the part of Don Lee surely went into its compilation, for "many of these volumes were published in limited editions," and several "were distributed on a regional basis" only.[19] Such a listing of available "primary sources" as this should prove to be of inestimable value to future Black critics, for it will help them to locate the Black poems from which a viable Black aesthetic will gradually develop.

Dynamite Voices I is finally important, then, not just because it was the first number in a projected series of Black critical works. Nor does its value lie only in the critical judgments and ideas that it contains—although, as this examination has shown, many of those judgments and ideas are both sound and valuable. Perhaps the greatest value of the volume is that it may serve both as a kind of "model" and as a "sourcebook" for other critics of the new Black poetry. In fact, some of the tentative assertions made by Lee here—both with regard to Black poetry in general and with regard to specific Black poets—have already been explored more fully by other Black critics (like Stephen Henderson). Future explorations based on Lee's tentative discoveries in *Dynamite Voices I* should insure Lee's short volume of a permanent place of importance in the development of the Black aesthetic.

NOTES

1. Don L. Lee, "Black Poetry: Which Direction?" *Negro Digest,* XVII (Sept.-Oct., 1968), 31.
2. Darwin T. Turner, "An Introduction: Afro-American Literary Critics," *Black World,* XIX (July, 1970), 66-67.
3. Hoyt W. Fuller, "An Important Beginning" (in "Perspectives"), *Black World,* XX (Sept., 1971), 82.

4. See Emanuel's "General Editor's Note," in Don L. Lee's *Dynamite Voices I: Black Poets of the 1960's* (Detroit: Broadside Press, 1971), p. 11.

5. See Fuller's "An Important Beginning," 82.

6. See, for example, Kenneth J. Zahorski's review in *CLAJ*, XV (Dec., 1971), 257-259; Charlotte Wilhite's review in *Black World*, XXI (Dec., 1971), 52; 83-88; and Carolyn F. Gerald's (less enthusiastic) review in *Black World*, XXI (June, 1972), 52; 82-85.

7. Notable exceptions to this general truth are Sterling Brown's *The Negro in American Fiction* and his *Negro Poetry and Drama*, both of which appeared in 1937, and Saunders Redding's *To Make a Poet Black*, which was published in 1939.

8. Detroit: Broadside Press, 1970, p. 5.

9. See Barbour's collection *The Black Seventies* (Boston: Sargent, Porter, 1970)—which, incidentally, contains an essay by Lee entitled "Tomorrow Is Tomorrow If You Want One" (pp. 241-251).

10. See *From Plan to Planet, Life Studies: The Need for Afrikan Minds and Institutions* (Detroit: Broadside Press, 1973), p. 113.

11. This description of White poetry appears on p. 37; it is a quotation taken by Lee from some (anonymous?) pre-1971 review in the *Saturday Review*.

12. See, particularly, p. 17, pp. 53-61, and pp. 166-168 of Albert Murray's *The Omni-Americans: New Perspectives on Black Experience and American Culture* (New York: Outerbridge, 1970).

13. Page 33. These early arguments of Lee concerning the indebtedness of modern Black poetry to both Black music and Black speech have since been expanded by Stephen Henderson in his long "Introduction: The Forms of Things Unknown," *Understanding the New Black Poetry: Black Speech and Black Music as Poetic References* (New York, 1973), pp. 1-69.

14. Don L. Lee, "Black Poetics/for the many to come," *Don't Cry, Scream* (Detroit: Broadside Press, 1969), p. 15.

15. See Lee's introductory comments (in which he quotes "the African critic Mukhtarr Mustapha"), p. 24.

16. See note 6 above.

17. See, for example, Lee's comments on p. 24 of the present volume and his "Directions for Black Writers," *The Black Scholar*, I (Dec., 1969), in which he states:

We, as black poets, writers, essayists, historians and teachers, must move into the small volume direction: small compact volumes of poetry, of essays, of short stories, of historical notes and small novellas, small black works that can be put into the back pockets and purses, volumes that can be conveniently read during the 15 minute coffee break or during the lunch hour (p. 55).

18. See Evans's poem "Speak the Truth to the People," which appears in Stephen Henderson's *Understanding the New Black Poetry: Black Speech and Black Music as Poetic References.* pp. 253-254.

19. See Gerald's review in *Black World,* p. 85. (See note 6 above.)

CHAPTER III

Perspectives for Change:
The Social Essays of Don L. Lee

When considering the latest volume by Don L. Lee, *From Plan to Planet*[1] (a collection of social essays), it is important to bear in mind, first, that an "essay" is an often highly utilitarian composition having no pretensions to completeness or thoroughness in its treatment of its subject. One must also remember that a "social essay" is even slightly more restricted in scope; it is an attempt (i.e., *essai*) to examine, seriously (even if somewhat incompletely or tentatively), some significant *social* issue—usually with the dual intention of exposing an existing problem and suggesting some solution(s) to that problem. In the social essay the "literary" end, or effect, holds a secondary position of importance; the essayist's primary concern is the social one, and his main emphasis is on *content*, not *form*.[2] That is, he is primarily concerned with moving his readers to rectify those social ills that he lays bare before them—not with pleasing their aesthetic palates with "polite, meaningless words."

Such a form seems, for many reasons, to be an almost inevitable choice for Don Lee, who had, in 1971, "agree[d] with the African critic Mukhtarr Mustapha" that:

> [The present] revolutionary state has compelled the writer to search extensively for the most laconic way of stating his case. The writers today in Africa and America are propelled by a desire for condensed expression, the writer's screening time is limited; therefore his task should be levelled toward clarity of thought in short forms.[3]

Lee had, moreover—in his even earlier "author's preface" to *Don't Cry, Scream* (1969)—asserted that even the primary function of "Blackpoetry" is to "tell what is *to be* & how to *be* it."[4] If the primary end of even Black *poetry* is social, then surely the traditionally short, pragmatic, analytical social essay form was made to order for Black Nationalists like Lee who believe, with Maulana Ron Karenga, that all art, like all educational institutions, should have "social content"—or else it "is of no importance at all."[5]

The possibility of using the social essay as a vehicle for liberation in the present-day Black Nationalist Movement was, in fact, early recognized by one of the acknowledged leaders of that Movement, Imamu Amiri Baraka (LeRoi Jones). Hence, writing in 1966 in "Philistinism and the Negro Writer," Baraka asserted that

> Negro literature has always been, in America, direct social response, which is, I think, the best kind of literature. . . . When I say social art, I mean not only art that is art by anyone's definition but art that will tell you how man lives, or, at least, how he wanted to live.[6]

Baraka went on, in that essay, to praise both the social essays of James Baldwin—particularly *Notes of a Native Son* (New York, 1955)—and Ralph Ellison's powerful social novel, *Invisible Man* (New York, 1952). That Baraka himself had long been aware of the liberating possibilities of social literature—in particular the social essay—is clear; for, in 1966 he also published his own first collection of social essays, *Home: Social Essays,* a volume containing essays that he had written over the preceding six years (1960-65). Baraka's continuing faith in the social essay as a viable vehicle for Afrikan liberation is reflected in one of his recent volumes, *Raise, Race, Rays, Raze: Essays Since 1965* (New York: Random House, 1969).

Baraka's confidence in the social essay has been infectious among his fellow Black Nationalists. Since the appearance of *Home,* countless volumes of essays by aspiring Black liberators have poured forth from presses throughout this country. While some of these volumes have been rightly ignored, others have caused quite a sensation among thinkers—both Black and White.

Among the most useful, in terms of advancing/supporting the Black Nationalist Movement, have probably been such volumes as *Black Expression: Essays by and About Black Americans in the Creative Arts* (New York, 1969) and *The Black Aesthetic* (New York, 1972), both edited by Addison Gayle, Jr.; *The Black Situation* (New York, 1972), a collection of Gayle's own essays; *Black Poets and Prophets: The Theory, Practice, and Esthetics of the Pan-Africanist Revolution,* edited by Woodie King and Earl Anthony (New York, 1972); and the two *Amistad* volumes [*Aimstad 1* (New York, 1970) and *Amistad 2* (New York, 1971)] edited by John A. Williams and Charles F. Harris. With the appearance of *From Plan to Planet,* Don Lee has joined the swelling ranks of significant Black social essayists.

The overriding concern of Don Lee in *From Plan to Planet* is the problem of Black survival. Echoing the concern of other Black leaders like Imamu Baraka and Samuel F. Yette,[7] Lee, speaking as "an Afrikan in America," asserts that the key to Afrikan survival (throughout the diaspora, but particularly in America)

> lies in our ability to produce a secure, competent, work-oriented, incorruptible generation of black men and women who will operate out of an Afrikan frame of reference based upon a proven black value system that incorporates a sense of Afrikan love and responsibility (pp. 13-14).

And, with this ultimate goal in mind, Lee projects in *From Plan to Planet* a multi-faceted "plan" that Black people in America and throughout the diaspora—for that matter, even in some parts of Afrika—can adopt, modify to meet their own immediate circumstances, and use to insure their survival—planet-wide. For his volume is, as Lee asserts,

> motivated toward the . . . building of Afrikan minds and institutions that will deal systematically and sensibly with the problems of Afrikan people while focusing on national/local struggles in relationship to the world struggle (p. 15).

The essays in *From Plan to Planet* are arranged into four

sections, and the final ordering of the sections themselves assumes some importance in terms of the overall effect of the volume. That is, there is a steady movement throughout the four sections that makes the final culminating effect of the volume greater than it would have been had the four sections been arranged differently. The first section, which is left untitled but which might well have been called either "An Afrikan Mind" or "Frame of Reference," examines the plight of the individual Black person—whatever his immediate locale—as he seeks to "*create* or *re-create* an Afrikan (or Black) mind in a *predominantly European-American setting*" (p. 45). Section two, which Lee calls "Life-Studies," shifts its focus from the problems facing the individual Black person to the problems of the local Black community, where Black persons of all types must learn to come together and work as a meaningful unit. From this examination of community problems, Lee moves, in section three ("The Black Arts"), to examine the interrelationships between the various Black communities in this country and to suggest different ways in which these geographically scattered Black communities might unite, psychologically, to form a vital Black nation. The role of the artist—as a forger of this Black nation—is examined in some detail in this third section. Section four, "Worldview," moves to encompass the international Black community; that is, in this section Lee suggests ways of adapting his earlier individual-community-national "plan" to the Black community worldwide (i.e., to the "planet").

From Plan to Planet is, clearly, an extremely ambitious book. And, to a large degree, Don Lee is successful in what he attempts in the volume. There are flaws—some serious, others relatively minor—in the volume, but the overall effect of the work is, as the following examination will show, very positive. Don Lee succeeds, for the most part, in his stated goal: he gives "*identity, purpose,* and *direction*" (p. 47) to Afrikan people.

In the first section of the book, which I will call "An Afrikan Mind," Lee asserts that one of the major problems facing most Black people today is their lack of positive identity. Failing to see themselves as "Afrikans" (whatever their current nation of dispersal), most Blacks have taken on "local definition[s]"; that is, they define themselves as "West Indian, Guyanese, French-Indian, Afro-European, etc." (p. 26). Consequently, "most Afrikans in America have become, after four hundred years of training, 'european-Americans' in thought, action, mannerisms, outlook, beliefs, and functional values" (p. 45). Such varied self-definitions as those currently used among widely dispersed Afrikans are a strong deterrent to Black survival, argues Lee; for only through asserting his oneness with all members of the Afrikan group can any Black person—anywhere—hope for meaningful survival. Only an "Afrikan" self-definition will effectively

> reinforce each [Afrikan's] . . . own sense of purpose and historical necessity. By associating oneself with a particular culture, a particular history and a particular land base, one's sense of identity and direction can be clarified in terms of a people's own best interest, vis-a-vis their enemies and the world (*From Plan to Planet*, p. 26).

And, in this first section, Lee outlines his plan for the creation of Afrikan minds.

The key to the creation of young Black minds is held by Black educators, according to Lee; for

> Either [Black] . . . people prepare their youth to be responsible and responsive to their *own needs* as a people or somebody else will teach them to be responsible and responsive to somebody else's needs at the expense and detriment of themselves and their people (p. 30).

But the existing problem of non-Black minds on the part of students is often only compounded by *Black-skinned* "European-American" teachers. Such teachers "[walk] the danger course and [carry] young minds with them. The only identity they [have is] . . . of themselves as individuals, and reflections of European-Americans" (p. 58). These teachers, although they have the Black *color* (i.e., pigmentation), lack Black "*culture and consciousness*" (p. 36); moreover, they are not *sound*, nor *serious,* nor *committed* to the issue of Black survival (p. 55). They are in fact a detriment to the cause: neither "responsible" nor "responsive" to the Black community, these teachers feather their own nests with their earnings, are concerned only with their individual desires.[8]

Such *Black-skinned* teachers as the foregoing are largely responsible for "the Failure of Black Studies" on college campuses, according to Lee (see pp. 55-61), and they—plus their Black and White allies who mis-educate in the Black primary, secondary, and post-secondary schools of this country—are strongly denounced by Lee. White faculty members have no place at all in the Black school system, asserts Lee; for "No European can create an Afrikan mind. Only a Afrikan can do that" (p. 45). Lee's rejection, here, of all White teachers closely echoes Maulana Karenga's similar sentiments expressed at the controversial Yale conference on "Black Studies in the University," in 1968. Here Karenga asserted that Whites must practice a policy of "nonintervention . . . in the black community" and in all Black institutions:

> What [Whites] . . . have to understand is that [they] . . . cannot intervene in the black community. [They] . . . don't really have any role in the [Black] community.[9]

Karenga's insistence on White nonintervention in Black educational institutions was based, of course, upon his clear understanding of the essentially *political* nature of all educational institutions. And Don Lee shares Karenga's belief that

> the educational institution has traditionally been, and is now, one of the institutions that the power structure maintains, in order to reinforce its own position.[10]

Consequently, only Black—in color, culture, and consciousness —educators can properly educate Black youth, can effectively shape Afrikan minds.[11]

Even Black educators cannot work in "a vacuum," however, asserts Lee: "We need structure. Before you can institutionalize *thoughts* and *actions,* you need institutions" (*From Plan to Planet,* p. 45). And such institutions—particularly Black schools —must be "independent black institutions"; that is, they must be "independent (void of outside control and influence), Black (in color, culture and consciousness)," and they must provide "a structured program aimed at correcting a deficiency, [by] giving concrete alternatives" (p. 39). It is not enough that students emerge from Black institutions with the "color and desire" (p. 50) to be Black: they must—if future generations of Afrikans in America are to survive—have learned certain technical skills; they must share a common Black value system; and they must feel a definite sense of oneness, or community, with other Black people throughout the world.

In "Life-Studies," the second section of *From Plan to Planet,* Lee examines the proper role of the Black individual, in relation to the local Black community in which that person functions. Since most Black people do lack the proper frame of reference, as Lee showed convincingly in "An Afrikan Mind," they are, for the most part, inhibited from functioning to the best advantage of themselves and other Black people. Essentially insecure, due to their habitual definition of themselves from a White (hence, anti-Black) frame of reference, most Blacks try to mask their insecurity by surrounding themselves with material evidences of their essential "worth." For example, as Lee points out in "Money, Power, Sex: The European-American Corruptibles," when a Black person begins to earn a substantial salary, he often "changes . . . [his] whole life style . . . to a level 'worthy' of [his] . . . new found riches." These "very superficial exterior" evidences of one's "worth"—big cars, fancy clothes, fabulous homes, and the like—really have nothing at all to do with one's essential "value," however; for human "worth" is an intrinsic, not an external, thing. Lee's own awareness of this truth is mirrored in his lament that, too often, Black people, "In our bid to be 'somebody' . . . [become] 'something' and are playing games" with little meaning (p. 76).

The desire of Black people for "individual success," which has repeatedly come under attack by Lee, almost from the

beginning of his career as a writer, is divisive and unnatural. Black people must, Lee argues, "out of survival-
necessity" (p. 75), begin to develop a strong group consciousness:

> There is no individual anything. The entire European/capitalist
> philosophy of the worth of the individual over the collective
> body is always the major stumbling-block when trying to build
> black community organizations (p. 67).

The Black value system that Lee suggests as a meaningful alternative to the divisive and destructive White value system that
most Blacks now subscribe to is the *Nguzo Saba* (as developed
by Maulana Ron Karenga), the Seven Principles of which
effectively prescribe an entire "way of life" for Black people.[12]
Underlying every principle of the *Nguzo Saba* is the essential
question: "Is it best for [all] Black People?" By continually
asking himself this question *before* he acts, a Black person will
automatically move away from concentrating on his own personal success to being concerned, foremost, with the good of
"the collective body" of Blacks (pp. 67-68).

The *Nguzo Saba* (part of Karenga's larger doctrine of
Kawaida), emphasizes the importance of revitalizing the traditional links between Black people throughout the diaspora and
those in the motherland, Afrika. While traditional Afrikan cultural values and institutions are given considerable significance
within this framework, Lee is not at all advocating the whole-
sale acceptance and revival of age-old (and sometimes out-
moded) Afrikan customs by technologically aware Black people
of the late twentieth century. Although Lee and other Black
Nationalists are often criticized for their desire to move Black
people back into an idyllic—and idealized—pre-technological
era, critics who accuse the Black Nationalists of this are largely
indicating their own ignorance with regard to the Black Nationalists' position on Afrikan culture. From the beginning Karenga,
Baraka, Lee and others have argued, essentially, that:

> We draw from tradition our cultural foundation of values and
> institutions. But we realize that we cannot . . . seek to return

to a totally Afrikan past while being both in America as well as in the present . . . . therefore, we must adjust our traditions to fit and facilitate our movement in America.[13]

Moreover, such critics of the Black Nationalist position again show their own lack of awareness concerning the essential nature of Afrikan customs on the continent itself. Afrikan customs are, and have always been, constantly changing, adapting themselves to ever-changing conditions. While these changes have been accelerated in areas plagued by dense colonialist intrusion, they have occurred, at a slower rate, throughout Afrika.

The *Nguzo Saba* is intended to be a communal "code" that Black people can live by. As Baraka points out elsewhere, this value system consists

> of spiritual concepts & scientific principles embodied as a morality system—complete in itself. . . .
> The 7 [sic] principles are '10 commandments' yet more profound to us—US because they are pre and post 10 commandments at the same time.[14]

As something that Black people everywhere should "study and adjust to," the *Nguzo Saba* provides a workable schema for "the unification and empowerment of Afrikan people" (p. 82); that is, it will lead, finally, to the Black community's being able to "produc[e] and distribut[e] . . . goods and services for [itself]" (p. 77). It places considerable emphasis on the re-creation of essentially Afrikan institutions through what Lee calls the "four basic ingredients . . . Work, Study, Creativity and Building."[15] Additionally, the *Nguzo Saba* encourages Black communities to be self-reliant, to found—and fund—their own Black institutions. Accordingly, on pages 84-85, Lee offers several "suggestions for internal funding" of Black institutions. Here he emphasizes the need for widespread cooperation—rather than competition—among Black businessmen. Through cooperative business enterprises and through the constant reinvestment of business profits within the Black community, Black businessmen can become an important unifying and strengthening force within that community.

Other potential forces for community development are the various Black professionals. Currently, Lee argues, a larger number of Black professionals are reneging on their community responsibilities than meeting their responsibilities. Lee addresses himself directly to this problem and confronts, first, the Black educator for his failure to be both responsible and responsive to the real needs of the Black community. Having reintroduced this problem (which he dealt with to some extent in "An Afrikan Mind"), Lee then offers what is, essentially, a "code of responsible conduct" for both teachers and students in the Black community (see pp. 68-69; p. 74). Moving from the Black educator to the Black medical doctor, Lee makes the following charges:

> There are the 'brothers' who doctor in the community and live in another world. For example, through the use of medicaid and regular practice some of these 'black' doctors net around $75,000 a year (p. 86).

Rather than suggesting guidelines for doctors' behavior similar to the educators' guidelines cited above, Lee focuses most of his attention on the responsibility of each Black person to try to avoid sickness in the first place; that is, Lee builds an essay around the concept of *preventive*—rather than *curative*—medicine.[16]

Many of the medical problems faced by Black people result, at least indirectly, from the widespread insecurity of Blacks in America, argues Lee. Lacking self-confidence and desiring to "fit in" in racist America, Blacks stay "hip" to foods that have "been sanctioned by ABC, CBS and NBC or some black entertainer with a crown on his head" (p. 87). This is true not only of foods but also of clothes, cars, household furnishings, types of entertainment, etc. Such behavior is not only futile but also harmful, Lee argues—in almost every case. Blacks who succumb to the (rather unhealthy) "standard" European-American diet, like those who succumb to the other "European-American Corruptibles" (money, power, sex), are certainly *not* doing what is best—either for themselves or for other Black

people—in the long run. According to Lee, just the reverse
is true; that is, "To abstain from certain foods not only disciplines
you internally, but mentally too, makes you quicker and sharper"
(p. 88). Similarly, to abstain from indulging in "luxuries" and
to content yourself with merely satisfying your *real* "needs"
(p. 76) is not only "logical and traditional" (p. 89); it also
enables you to focus most of your energies toward effecting
what really *is* "best for [all] Black people" (p. 67).

Section two ends with the extremely short essay "Ain't No
Drug Problem in the Italian Community" (p. 89). Here Lee
suggests that, although cohesiveness and communal spirit exist
within Italian communities, these same qualities are missing from
most Black communities. Any reader of Lee's volume will
surely be aware that there *is* an extreme drug problem in the
Black community, and he will also likely be aware that the
Italian Mafia is often charged with being responsible for much
of the existing drug traffic in Black communities. Yet, group-
interest—as opposed to the drug pusher's economic self-interest
—successfully keeps the drug problem out of the Italian community, says Lee. The point Lee is making in this essay is
clear: Italians prey upon others (non-Italians), not upon themselves; their actions are determined by the principle of "Is it
best for the *Italian* community?" This final brief essay performs
two functions, then: (1) it again points up the present dis-
unity in the Black community (where most drugs are probably
still sold); and (2) it shows how extremely effective a group-
oriented value system (rather than an individual-oriented one)
can be in terms of group welfare and/or advancement.

Lee moves from his analysis, in "Life-Studies," of the
problems faced by the local Black community to treat, in
section three ("The Black Arts"), many of those same problems,
most of which exist on an even larger scale, within the emerging
Black nation. If the local Black community is kept divided by
Black individuals who lack "*identity, purpose, or direction*"
(p. 48), then the same is surely true of the larger Black nation,
argues Lee. Hence, he concentrates most of his efforts in this
third section towards making specific recommendations which,

if followed, will enable the Black nation to become a reality—
will help it to become both "autonom[ous] and self sufficien[t]"
(p. 117). The key to molding the presently disorganized Black
people of this country into a powerful Black nation is held,
according to Lee, by "Black 'artists' (image-makers—writers,
photographers, film makers, dancers, musicians, actors, workers
in the plastic arts, etc.)" (p. 92). Such is true, Lee is convinced, because the most "subtle drug" of all those that are
currently being used in the Black community as a deterrent
to nation building is "the image. He who controls the image
controls the mind" (p. 102). The only way, then, that the
Black nation can become a reality is for Black artists to work
together "to re-direct, and re-define, or re-focus [Black] minds."[17]

In the poem that opens this third section, Lee once again
contrasts the strong communal sense and the group-oriented
efforts of other U.S. "minority groups" (in this case Jews and
Irishmen) with the lack of group-identity that Black people
evince. For all of the "bad-mouthing" of Whites that the most
widely known "militant black writers" engage in, says Lee,
most of them actually *do* very little to help their people advance
as a group/nation. Rather, they publish their books with White
publishing houses, and the profits from the books of these
"militant black writers" are used to perpetuate White supremacy
—worldwide, not just in the U.S. For those Whites who publish
the "militant black writers" send their (very large) share of
the profits "to Israel and Ireland to build a nation for" Jews
and Irishmen (p. 91). What is true of Black writers is also true,
in varying degrees, of other Black artists; Black artists as a
whole

> lack . . . power and final control over our own 'art' form . . . ;
> [we also] . . . lack . . . concrete direction or purpose, that is
> we're all creators for different 'personal' reasons and therefore
> only feel we are accountable to ourselves as pseudo individuals
> and not to black people as a body (p. 92).

Many of the complaints leveled at Black artists—particularly
writers and musicians—will be quite familiar to readers of

Lee's poetry. They are, moreover, closely related to the charges made earlier in this present volume against "educated [Black] pimps" (p. 57) and "the new 'black' poverty or 'ghetto' doctors" (p. 86). The "crimes" that these artists, educators, and doctors are charged with are two: (1) they are either ignorant of, or else they ignore (because they are motivated by the desire for personal profit), the fact that "everything in this country is political, from the drug addiction of a thirteen year old to the illiteracy of a grown man" (p. 133); (2) they are not "sound," "serious," or "committed" (p. 55); hence, they fail to provide positive *identity, purpose,* or *direction*" (p. 48) to the Black community. This is particularly harmful in the case of Black artists, however; for, despite the frequent lack of understanding of, and commitment to solving, the problem of Black survival on the part of the Black artist, the Black community/nation continues to "get quite a few [of its priorities] from the black 'artist' " (p. 93). As a result, the noncommitted (or self-committed) Black artist is, Lee declares, "just as dangerous as the dope pusher" (p. 102), for he ultimately causes even greater psychological dis-unity in the Black community than existed before.

Attempting to reorder the priorities of misdirected Black artists—so that these artists can, in turn, properly direct their Black audiences—Lee spends much of this third section making various concrete proposals concerning how Black artists can come together "to organize, mobilize and institutionalize needed change at the mass level" (p. 105). More than anything else, the following three things are needed, says Lee:

(1) "a national black communications conference. . . . [that] would bring together brothers and sisters from all spectrums of the communications field" (p. 93) so that, through serious discussion, the proper—and essentially *political*—role of the Black artist in the Black community would be better understood by Black artists.

(2) an organization of Black musicians, which would concern itself with the "common needs and problems" of *all* Black musicians. This organization would focus especially on "the economic and business side of their profession" (p. 100),

which too few Black musicians seem to understand adequately.

(3) cooperative efforts between Black publishers of and distributors of works by Black artists. This teamwork is essential, argues Lee, for "mass distribution is the major necessity in the success of a book other than the quality of the book itself" (p. 117). Working together as a unit, "each publisher [would] push and solicit sales for all the . . . Combined Black Publishers." Moreover, these publishers would push "not only [Black] books, but records, tapes, pamphlets, posters and broadsides" (p. 118) in Black communities throughout the nation.

Such proposals as these, if followed, would not only flood the various Black communities in America with positive Black self-images but would also keep both the control of Black art and the monies acquired from the sale of Black art within the hands of members of the Black community/nation. And, as Lee points out repeatedly in this section, with this new wealth would come new *real* power for Blacks in America.

In the final ("Worldview") section of *From Plan to Planet* Lee moves to confront what he considers the largest single problem that Black people, worldwide, have. This problem is, essentially, a kind of naiveté concerning (1) *how* the world is really run, and (2) *who* really runs the world. This naiveté must be overcome, Lee argues, for "One must [first] understand and be able to define the enemy in order to systematically deal with him" (p. 100). Moreover,

hopefully, by analyzing our problem locally, nationally, and internationally once and for all, without fear we'll recognize that the world's enemy, not just the Afrikan's enemy, is the European (p. 43).

In the preceding three sections of this volume, Lee has dealt with the "local" and the "national" (as well as with the "individual") problem(s) of Black people, and in this final section he completes his schema, as he carefully examines the motives, methods, and ends of the European-American worldrunners.

First Lee traces, historically, the Europeans' and the European-Americans' struggles to impose both a European (White) frame of reference and a White value system on large numbers of colonized peoples throughout the world—particularly in Afrika—"under the guise of bringing democratic civilization and Christian enlightenment to the 'savages'" (p. 123). Such "unnatural" acts by the White people of the world can be understood, Lee argues, only when one considers the actual position of Whites (or, as Lee calls them, "non-coloreds") in the world: comprising a mere thirteen percent of the world's population, Whites, motivated by both fear (of survival) and, perhaps, self-disgust (since they seemed to be "unnatural" in an otherwise "colored" world), sought—and managed, usually through violent means—to impose both a European frame of reference and a White value system on most of the "colored" peoples of the world. Consequently, from being insecure psychological "misfits" in an otherwise "colored" world, Whites became, in the minds of all who functioned from this European frame of reference and according to this White value system, a "superior" race (pp. 137-142).[18] Lee goes on to carefully point out that European control of Afrika did *not* end with the "'paper' independence" (p. 125) of many Afrikan nations in the 1950s and 1960s. Rather, final control of most of Afrika remains in the hands of Europeans—as do the "titles" to enormous portions of Afrikan land (pp. 126-127). The only way that Afrika can truly become "for Afrikan people" (p. 128) is through unified,

> deliberate and systematic action with black purpose and direction underscored with the major impetus that is required in any peoples' struggle—the love of a people for self (p. 129).

Love, then, holds a position of supreme importance in the reordering of Afrikan minds and Afrikan priorities. In attesting to this fact, Lee is merely echoing the earlier assertations of Julius K. Nyerere, who, in his *Ujamaa: Essays on Socialism*, often points out that "love" is essential to successful group-living (or even group-consciousness). This is true because "love" implies "a recognition of mutual involvement in one another,"[19] or, in Lee's terms, love gives "identity, purpose, and direction" to the *group.* There is one major difference, however, between Lee's concept of *ujamaa,* or "familyhood" based on love, and that advanced by Nyerere. Nyerere, throughout *Ujamaa: Essays on Socialism,* continually reiterates his belief that

> socialism and racism are incompatible. . . . the man or woman who hates 'Jews', or 'Asians', or 'Europeans', or even 'West Europeans and Americans' is not a socialist. He is trying to divide mankind into groups and is judging men according to the[ir] skin colour. . . . In [any] . . . case he is denying the equality and brotherhood of man.
>
> Without an acceptance of human equality there can be no socialism (p. 39).

Moreover, when speaking of nationbuilding, Nyerere declares that nationbuilders must focus upon *issues,* not upon *people:*

> To try and divide up the people working for our nation into groups of 'good' and 'bad' according to their skin colour, or their national origin, or their tribal origin, is to sabotage the work we have just embarked upon (p. 41).

Don Lee does pay lip service, briefly, to Nyerere's view of love; for example, he comments that

> Our struggle should not be based upon the *hate* of anything. . . . One cannot build a movement on the negative. . . . Our fight . . . should not be anti[-]European-Americans, anti-capitalism or anti-white, but should be pro-Pan-Afrikanism, pro-Ujamaa (Co-Operative Economics) and pro-black people (p. 132).

Much of *From Plan to Planet,* however, clearly contradicts these "anti-negativism" comments: White people have, throughout the essays in this volume, been seen as not just "the Afrikan's enemy" but also "the world's enemy" (p. 43).

There are, then, some inconsistencies in the volume concerning "the equality and brotherhood of *man.*" But, there are no such inconsistencies when Lee is talking about *Black* man— wherever he may be found (in Afrika or at any point in the diaspora). For Lee sees all Afrikans as being a part of one worldwide extended family. Such a "family" concept is essential to Black survival, says Lee; for, "You cannot solve a family problem when you're not even defined as a family." More importantly, "the extended family is the beginning of the extended organization" (pp. 134-135). And, from the extended organization comes the nation—from which, in turn, develops a cohesive international Black community. Although Lee's emphasis, here, is on Pan-Afrikanism, a logical extension of his "pro-colored" attitude would be "Third Worldism" or the uniting of all "colored" peoples in order to throw off the yoke of oppression by the "non-coloreds."

In the final essay in this collection, "Culture/Commitment/ Conclusions for Action," Lee again points out the need for Black people everywhere—but particularly those in the U.S.— to become "political, technological, and historical" (p. 143) if they are to survive and become the designers of their own tomorrows. That is, Black people must be aware of both where they are coming from and where they hope to move to; moreover, they must have various alternative plans for getting there. Lee has already indicated just how, in his estimation, the Europeans earlier became the "worldrunners" (p. 143); they had, according to Lee: (1) "a common value system . . . a national language . . . national cultural patterns"—all of which gave them "the necessary group and national consciousness"; (2) "common purpose" (i.e., the desire "to expand their empires," etc.); (3) technological knowledge—"especially in communication, transportation . . . and warfare"; (4) "modern organization"—particularly in the fields of "government, business, and the military" (pp. 124-125). Presumably, it is only by following some similar program that Afrikans will be able, in the foreseeable future, to "Re-tak[e] the Takeable" (p. 29) and determine their own destiny.

At the end of this volume, Lee includes what he calls a "Worldview . . . Reading List." This long list of books, which covers the final nine pages of *From Plan to Planet,* contains important studies that deal with each of the major problem areas of Black life. If these books—and others of each reader's own choice—are read and studied from the proper (Afrikan) frame of reference, they can prove extremely helpful in aiding the reader "to understand our life and death struggle" (p. 149), says Lee. They can, moreover, give direction to those who are—or would become—actively engaged in the worldwide struggle for Black liberation, by suggesting certain alternatives for action which the reader may, at present, be unaware of. These alternatives may, in turn, enable the reader to solve certain problems which have heretofore seemed to be insolvable.

The importance of sharing all knowledge is well understood by Lee, who asserts, in closing, that:

> The world is not only controlled by men with 'knowledge' but by men who mis-use 'knowledge' and to possess 'knowledge' and not use it for the betterment of Afrikan people is, in my value system, a mis-use (p. 149).

Lee himself shares much of his own knowledge with readers of *From Plan to Planet,* as he follows a fairly steady course of action in most of his essays. First he attempts to identify, or isolate, the particular problem that he wants to deal with in any essay; then he studies the problem, frequently trying to view it from more than one angle; finally he (usually) attempts to offer his readers some solution to the problem—or, at least, some alternative plan for coping realistically with that problem.

There are, however, numerous flaws in *From Plan to Planet.* While some of these flaws are of a relatively minor mechanical nature, others are of a more serious—and sometimes ideological —kind. In the area of mechanics, Lee makes a number of errors that can possibly be ascribed to mere carelessness: there are frequent spelling and punctuation errors, occasional confusing—or even garbled—sentences, incomplete footnotes, partially rendered statistics, and overused Black Nationalistic catch phrases. Popular phrases, moreover, often lead to hackneyed ideas, and some of Lee's essays suffer from a distinct lack of original ideas. More serious faults occur as Lee makes an occasional false appeal to authority or fails to suggest a workable solution to some problem that he is examining. Probably the most significant ideological weaknesses that occur in the volume are that Lee sometimes seems to see Whites as some kind of "Superbeings" (which occasionally causes him to fall into a heavily reactionary rhetoric of near-hysteria) and he occasionally sees himself and other Black Nationalists in almost that same "elite" role.

It would almost seem that the galley proofs for *From Plan to Planet* were not proofread, if one were to judge from the almost countless number of typographical errors that appear in the text. Practically any page will offer an illustration of spelling or punctuation errors like those that appear on page 100, where Lee says:

> However, at some point in a man'e [sic] life, it becomes not enough to keep blowing hot air at the *man;* when do we as responsible people begin to critically assess the collective problem we face. [sic]

Less frequent, fortunately, are sentences like the following:

> What concerns us about the *Report* is that it suggests that in order to control the "undesirables" or "potential enemies" of society, a given socety [sic] must consider "the re-introduction, in some form consistent with modern technology and political reality. [sic] (p. 60).

Although the reader is possibly undaunted by simple spelling errors by the time he has reached this point in the book, he is probably still considerably disturbed by Lee's apparently ending his quotation from the *Report* in mid-sentence and by his failing to "make sense" in his own statement. Any reader will almost surely be left wondering just *what* is to be "re-introduced" in order to "control the 'undesirables'" that Lee has been discussing.

A reader who is extremely curious about the matter has several "clues" he can follow, if he really wants to discover those words that have apparently been left out of Lee's sentence.

Lee has said already that the *Report* he is discussing is the *Report from Iron Mountain,* which "was published in 1967" (p. 60). While Lee has *not* given the number of the *page* from which his apparent misquotation was taken, a diligent querist can find it for himself. The intended quotation, when found, makes complete sense; it says:

> Another possible surrogate for the control of potential enemies of society is the reintroduction, in some form consistent with modern technology and political processes, *of slavery.*[20] (Emphasis my own.)

Lee has, then, either by originally misquoting his source or by later failing to carefully proofread his galleys, left out the "key" to this particular argument. Such carelessness as this certainly lessens the intended impact of the volume.

Other garbled sentences occur—too often—in *From Plan to Planet.* While a persistent reader can usually figure out what Lee *intended* to say, this is not always the case. Even the most diligent reader will probably be unable to figure out just exactly *what* Lee means in his first two paragraphs on page 49. The essay in question deals, ironically, with "Communications: The Language of Control," and the first paragraph that the reader *can* read opens with the (in this case almost damning) statement:

> The language you speak is just about synonymous with the culture you practice (p. 49).

The frequency of the (often rather significant) mechanical errors in this volume suggests both carelessness and a lack of consideration on the part of the author for his readers.

This suspicion of thoughtlessness is further augmented by Lee's usual haphazard and incomplete manner of documenting his quotations from other authors. Although Lee has a tendency to support his own often controversial assertions with statements made by other Black Nationalists, he seldom tells his reader where these supportive remarks first appeared in print. He habitually introduces both direct and indirect quotations from other sources with inadequate phrases like the following: "as Mwalimu Julius Nyerere suggests . . ." (p. 33); "according to Maulana [Karenga] . . ." (p. 35); "Paulo Freire has said that" (p. 39); "as Brother Sterling Plumpp has said" (p. 47); "John H. Clarke puts it this way" (p. 127). Lee very rarely gives even the *title* of the book that his quoted material appeared in, and he never gives a *page* reference. For readers who would like to explore Lee's controversial issues further, the incomplete documentation in *From Plan to Planet* offers little help in finding relevant materials. Though quotations abound throughout this volume, there are only *three* footnotes in the whole book (p. 45, p. 81, and p. 141), and even those footnotes are incomplete.

The impact of this volume is also occasionally lessened by Lee's incomplete quoting of statistics. For example, in "The New Pimps . . ." (pp. 55-61) Lee states that "fifty-five per cent of black people in this country now live in urban areas. In Chicago where over a million of us exist, we're confined to less than twelve per cent of the land" (p. 60). Although this statement is, within itself, damning (of the White Establishment), it would probably have been even *more* damning if Lee had pointed out what percentage of the population of Chicago is Black. The reader is left wondering: "Do Black people constitute fifty-five percent of Chicago's population? Are they more than that? Are they less than that? Is Lee talking about only metropolitan Chicago, or does he also include the suburbs in these figures?" Don Lee does not say.

As indicated above, Lee frequently quotes from other sources. He also, unfortunately, depends far too heavily on what many recent critics have called the rhetorical slogans of Black Nationalism.[21] One essay that loses much of its force as a result of the constant repetition of certain italicized Black Nationalistic catch phrases is "Institutions: From Plan to Planet" (pp. 43-48). Here Lee indulges his passion for repeating such italicized slogans as the following:

(1) *"identity, purpose, and direction"* (p. 44, p. 47, p. 48)

(2) *"consciousness . . . commitment,* and *. . . actions"* (p. 44)
(3) *"color, culture,* and *consciousness"* (p. 44, p. 48)
(4) *"awareness, acceptance,* and *practice"* (p. 47).

Lee apparently uses this technique in an attempt to make certain positive slogans stick in his reader's mind. Many readers, however, will probably object to this constant sloganizing. And they may suspect Lee of both laziness and a lack of originality in his phrase-making.

Lee's frequent use of hackneyed phrases causes the reader to be relatively unsurprised when in the entire first section of *From Plan to Planet* he encounters almost no new *ideas*—or even new arrangements of old ideas. Most of the essay entitled "Institutions: From Plan to Planet" is, in fact, little more than a hodgepodge of the earlier ideas of other Black Nationalists—in particular the ideas of Maulana Ron Karenga, Imamu Amiri Baraka, and Johari Amini. Such essays as this one make Lee's earlier assertion that "I believe that much of what is written has been written before; much of what is said has been said before" (p. 15) seem indeed like an understatement. Fortunately, as the volume progresses, the number of new ideas that Lee has also increases.

In what may be an attempt to make some of his more audacious positions on particular issues seem to be prevalent ones, Lee sometimes falsely appeals to authority. Perhaps the most obvious instance of this occurs in the essay "Money, Power, Sex: The European-American Corruptibles" (pp. 74-78), where Lee opens with the following quotation from "Osagyefo Kwame Nkrumah":

> women, money, organized and obligatory religion, all three of them represent to my mind something that should play a minor part in man's life, for once one of them gets the upper hand, man becomes a slave and his personality is crushed.

Although Lee himself declares that "Osagyefo, in his usual down to earth manner, again hits at the core of our many problems" (p. 74), he goes on to develop his essay *not* around the "dangerous excesses" identified by Nkrumah (who seems to be merely making a plea for moderation) but around his own designated "European-American Corruptibles"—"money, power, sex." The reader is left wondering, "Why this difference? Why is Nkrumah's list of personal excesses both changed somewhat and given *racial* implications?" Although the differences between these two lists of things to avoid seem rather significant to the reader, Lee makes no attempt to explain the disparity; rather, he seems to be completely unaware that his position is not identical with that of Nkrumah. At least he totally ignores the difference. This quotation from Nkrumah does not, then, actually support Lee's thesis—even though, judging from its position in the essay, it was evidently meant to do so. It is, in fact, rather irrelevant to the essay itself. Consequently, Lee seems to be little more than name-dropping in an attempt to add "official" support to his own position.

When confronting some of the problems that he deals with in this volume, Lee seems to be unable to come up with any very practicable solution to those problems. Occasionally an essay will lack the final positive suggestion that, yes, Black people probably *can* do something about the situation described in the essay. Those essays that fail to offer at least some tentative workable solution to the problem under examination lack the positive force of the others. Perhaps the most negative essay in *From Plan to Planet,* in this respect, is "Are Black Musicians Serious?" (pp. 99-103). Here Lee confronts the complex problem of "other people market[ing] our music . . . mak[ing] nightmares of our dreams . . . [and] misus[ing] the songs of our fathers" (p. 99). After moving through a multi-level attack on "the black musician . . . [who] has to always do his *thang* at the expense of the group and sometimes the nation itself" (p. 101), Lee concludes "that a people must control its art—if it is to re-direct, and re-define, or re-focus minds" (p. 103); yet, he hardly presents this solution as a real possibility. His final assessment of Black musicians is that they are probably at least one of the following:

1) extremely naive, 2) totally ignorant and receiving bad advice, 3) just outright treacherous and would do anything for himself or herself [sic] at the expense of everybody else (p. 102).

Such musicians as these would seem highly unlikely candidates for controlling their own—or anybody else's—art. And Lee himself almost seems to dismiss this possibility when, in his final statement, he suggests,

we deserve to be in the position that we're in (p. 103).

Since he sees Black people as frequently being in a "position" that is somehow "lower" than that of Whites ("the World-runners"), Lee tends, occasionally, to view Whites from what Richard Wright has elsewhere called "frog perspective." That is, Lee sometimes seems to be

looking from below upward [at Whites. He seems to have] a sense of . . . [being] lower than [Whites]. . . . The concept of distance involved here is not physical; it is psychological. . . . A certain degree of hate combined with love (ambivalence) is always involved in this looking from below upward and the object against which the subject is measuring himself undergoes constant change. He loves the object because he would like to resemble it; he hates the object because his chances of resembling it are remote, slight.[22]

A hint of "frog perspective" seems clear in the essay referred to above ("Are Black Musicians Serious?"), and it also occurs on page 61, where Lee asserts:

We have enough leaders leading us no place. And yes, we know that we're a bad people; we so bad that we badly organized, badly situated and badly taught as we loosely talk about nation-building like its [sic] something that will jump out of the sky. If the white boy gave us a block tomorrow, we'd have problems running and organizing it.

Such self- and group-denigrating comments as these certainly lessen the positive force of *From Plan to Planet*.

"Frog perspective" may also account for at least some of Lee's occasional clamorous attacks on Whites. One such attack occurs in the middle of the essay "Where Are the Black Educators Who Are Educated Blackly?" (pp. 35-41) as Lee digresses for two pages to indulge in a series of near-hysterical questions and assertions. Having stated that most U.S. Blacks are naive about "how the *world* works," that they focus on local rather than on international problems, Lee demands, "What about Afrika? What about South America? What about other parts of Asia?" Then follows a long list of "We have to begin to understand. . . . We . . . have to understand. . . . We need to understand. . . ." (p. 36). Just what it is that "we have to understand" becomes clear in a long paragraph running from the bottom of page 36 to page 38, where Lee lays the blame for all Black problems at the feet of "European-Americans! European-Americans who know. . . . Who does this? Americans and Europeans! *Who* . . . ? . . . . Who . . . ? . . . . Who . . . ? . . . ." Always the answer is the same: "Again European-Americans" (p. 37).

Such an "inventory of the bad habits"[23] of Whites as the above recalls other similar vociferous charges of "White evil" that characterized Lee's first two (highly reactionary) volumes of poetry. In that respect, parts of *From Plan to Planet* mark an ideological "step backward" from the confident positivism of both *Don't Cry, Scream* (1969) and, particularly, *We Walk the Way of the New World* (1970). Moreover, such an "inventory" really has little positive value at this point. Although Lee's *facts* in this instance are indisputable, the force with which he presents these facts tends to overwhelm his reader, to make him fear to oppose such all-powerful worldrunners as Lee has described.

Lee's reader (presumably himself a potential Black liberator) may also be discouraged by a number of passages that reflect a rather elitist posture on the part of Lee. For example, on page 15 Lee says:

> The frustration that conscious black men and women undergo in this country is nothing less than extraordinary. The psychological

stress and strain that the West puts on us (depending upon our consciousness) is vast, and for us to remain sane and politically active under such weight is a phenomenon of the mind and body.

Such elitist comments as these would tend, it seems, to deter the potential Black liberator from attempting to expand his consciousness; for, the greater the consciousness, the greater the attendant pain. Even if he were willing to accept the pain—in return for the awareness—however, such a potential revolutionary reads a little farther only to discover that only "exceptional brothers and sisters" can even *hope* to cope with the White Establishment (p. 52). If he sees himself as merely an "ordinary" young person, again the prospective Black nation-builder is deterred.

All of the flaws in this volume—from the most minor mechanical ones to the most major ideological ones—suggest to the reader that this volume was possibly put together in great haste (even *despite* Lee's assurance that he worked on the manuscript over a two-year period [p. 14]). These flaws do not, however, negate the real value of the book. For the work is, as Lee himself points out in his early "Comments," "a groundbreaking work" (p. 15) in many ways. These essays show that Don Lee clearly has both the perspicacity to identify and the courage to directly confront many of the most serious problems facing Black people today. Such perspicacity and courage are sorely needed in the worldwide struggle for Black liberation. Moreover, many of the essays in this volume are marked by neither ideological nor serious mechanical flaws.

Some of the essays collected here offer sharply focused, incisive examinations of problem areas that have been left largely unexplored by most Black writers to date. Perhaps the most impressive essay, in this regard, is "The Necessity of Control: Publishing to Distribution" (pp. 115-120), in which Lee makes "A Short Proposal for Black Distributors" (p. 115) which, if acted upon, would certainly net far-reaching positive returns for Black people in America. Another particularly valuable essay is "Mwalimu/Mwanafunzi Relationship (Teacher/Student)" (pp. 68-74), in which Lee proposes a "behavioral code" for both Black teachers and Black students. This essay is even illustrated with pictures showing successful Black teachers and students at work—in the New Concept School in Chicago (see pp. 70-73).

Lee's rather careful organization of these essays into four complementary sections helps to leave the reader with the feeling that practically all of the major Black problems have at least been "touched on" by Lee in the course of his study. Lee moves, honestly and fairly steadily, from dealing with the problems that confront Black individuals, through confronting those that are community-wide and nation-wide, to treating those that face Black people wherever they are (i.e., international problems). In assessing both the problems faced by Blacks and the causes of these various problems, as well as in suggesting possible "cures" for the Black dilemma, Lee has written a volume that demands the undivided attention of all potential Black liberators. Moreover, if the multi-faceted "plan" proposed by Lee in these essays were followed by Black people, and if this plan were supplemented by others of the various plans that are listed at the end of the volume (in the "Worldview . . . Reading List"), the (united) colored peoples of the world should not fail to

> . . . become owners of the   New World
> the New World.
> will run it as unowners
> for
> we will live in it too
> & will want to be remembered
> as   realpeople.[24]

NOTES

1. Don L. Lee, *From Plan to Planet, Life Studies: The Need for Afrikan Minds and Institutions* (Detroit: Broadside Press, 1973).

2. For a more detailed discussion of this genre, see C. Hugh Holman, *A Handbook to Literature,* 3rd ed. (New York: Odyssey Press, 1972).

3. Don L. Lee, *Dynamite Voices I: Black Poets of the 1960's* (Detroit: Broadside Press, 1971), p. 24.

4. Detroit: Broadside Press, 1969, p. 16.

5. See Maulana Ron Karenga, "The Black Community and the University: A Community Organizer's Perspective," in *Black Studies in the University*, ed. Armstead L. Robinson, Craig C. Foster, and Donald H. Ogilvie (New York: Yale Univ. Press, 1969), pp. 38-56; quotation appears on p. 42. Also see Karenga's "Black Cultural Nationalism," in *The Black Aesthetic*, ed. Addison Gayle, Jr. (New York: Doubleday, 1972), pp. 31-37.

6. This essay appears in *Anger and Beyond: The Negro Writer in the United States*, ed. Herbert Hill (New York: Harper-Row, 1966), pp. 51-61; see p. 57 for quoted material.

7. Imamu Baraka, in a talk on "Black Survival" given at Howard University on October 25, 1972, made many of the same points that Lee makes in this current volume. Samuel Yette, writing in *The Choice: The Issue of Black Survival in America* (New York: Putnam, 1971), did likewise.

8. Lee himself functions as both a "responsible" and a "responsive" Black educator in the classrooms of Howard University, where he has been Writer-in-Residence since fall, 1971.

9. *Black Studies in the University*, p. 38. (See above, note 5.)

10. *Black Studies in the University*, p. 39.

11. It is interesting to note that Paulo Freire, a noted Brazilian educator, although himself assured of the essentially political nature of educational institutions, nonetheless believes that former members of the "oppressor" group might meaningfully work at teaching/learning with the "oppressed." So convinced is Freire of this fact that he dedicated his revolutionary "handbook," *Pedagogy of the Oppressed*, trans. Myra Bergman Ramos (New York, 1972), "To the oppressed, / and to those who suffer with them / and fight at their side."

12. See "A Black Value System: Why the *Nguzo Saba?*" in *From Plan to Planet*, pp. 79-82.

13. *From Plan to Planet*, p. 79. (Quotation was taken from Karenga, by Lee.)

14. Imamu Amiri Baraka, *Kawaida Studies: The New Nationalism* (Chicago: Third World Press, 1972), p. 10.

15. See *From Plan to Planet*, pp. 64-66; quotation appears on p. 64.

16. See "The Natural Energy for Positive Movement," in *From Plan to Planet*, pp. 86-89.

17. *From Plan to Planet*, p. 103. Lee's emphasis, here, on the extreme importance of the role the Black artist plays in Black nationbuilding recalls other significant studies concerning the role of

Black professionals in nationbuilding. See, for example, Harold Cruse, *The Crisis of the Negro Intellectual* (New York: William Morrow, 1967); E. Franklin Frazier, *Black Bourgeoisie* (New York: Macmillan, 1957); Carter Godwin Woodson, *The Mis-Education of the Negro*, reissue (Washington, D.C.: The Association Publishers, Inc., 1969); and Frantz Fanon, *The Wretched of the Earth*. (See note 23.)

18. Lee's argument here was developed from an earlier theory on White racism advanced by Dr. Frances Cress Welsing, a child and general psychiatrist who is affiliated with the Howard University College of Medicine (Department of Pediatrics).

Dr. Welsing's theory was advanced in her booklet, *The Cress Theory of Color-Confrontation and Racism (White Supremacy): (A Psycho-Genetic Theory and World Outlook)* (Washington, D.C., 1970).

19. See, for example, Nyerere's "Socialism and Rural Development," in *Ujamaa: Essays on Socialism* (New York: 1968), p. 107. Also see his "The Purpose Is Man," pp. 91-105 of that same volume.

20. Leonard C. Lewin, *Report from Iron Mountain on the Possibility and Desirability of Peace* (New York: Dell, 1967), p. 70.

21. See, for example, Arthur P. Davis, "The New Poetry of Black Hate," *CLAJ*, XIII (June, 1970), 382-391 and Albert Murray, *The Omni-Americans: New Perspectives on Black Experience and American Culture* (New York: Outerbridge, 1970), pp. 153-157; p. 193; p. 206.

22. *White Man, Listen!* (New York: Anchor Books, 1964), p. 6.

23. Frantz Fanon, *The Wretched of the Earth*, trans. Constance Farrington, First Evergreen Black Cat Edition (New York, 1968), p. 221.

24. Don L. Lee, "We Walk the Way of the New World," in *We Walk the Way of the New World* (Detroit: Broadside Press, 1970), p. 66.

CHAPTER IV

Don L. Lee: Black Educator

"Where are the Black educators who are educated Blackly?" demands Don L. Lee in his recent volume of social essays, *From Plan to Planet*. Lee then goes on to argue that at present fewer than *one percent* of all the Black children in the United States are being educated by Black educators who (1) have not been "Americanized" out of their "Afrikanness" and (2) are fully accountable to the Black communities in which they work (and, presumably, live).[1] Lee's point, while possibly overstated, is nonetheless extremely important; there *is* a dearth of "Blackly educated" Black educators in America today. But: some *do* exist, and they *do* teach, and they *are* responsible to the Black communities in which they live and work. Such "real" Black educators as Lee describes in his essay may almost surely be found, at least in small numbers, in most areas where there is a highly concentrated Black population. There are, moreover, certain areas—Newark, Chicago, and Washington, D.C., for instance—where they abound. In these places one can, in fact, see entire—and usually closeknit—cadres of Black educators engaged in the business of educating Black students "Blackly"—at all educational levels.

At Howard University in Washington, D.C., for example, there may currently be found quite a large number of (often highly successful) Black educators, for Black Studies are quite actively supported by Howard's President James E. Cheek.[2] At Howard that radical "Black Power" movement of the late 1960s has, in fact, become fairly well institutionalized within the university structure itself. Not only are there fully staffed departments of both Afrikan and Afro-American Studies, but there are also a considerable number of Pan-Afrikanist teachers on the Howard faculty. Moreover, fairly regular speaking appearances are made by such visiting Pan-Afrikanist leaders as Imamu Baraka and Stokely Carmichael. Probably among the most successful of all the Black educators at Howard University is Don Lee himself, who has been "Writer-in-Residence" at Howard for the past two academic years (1971-1973). The purpose of this chapter is to describe how Don Lee functions as a Black educator: to discuss his goals, his methodology, and his manner as he conducts his classes; to examine, briefly, his extra-classroom teaching activities; to try to predict the eventual results of his teaching.[3]

Don Lee and his fellow Black educators (both at Howard University and elsewhere) can readily be distinguished from those "educated Black pimps" who are neither "sound" nor "serious" nor "committed"[4] to educating today's Black students "Blackly." For the real Black educator—unlike the educated pimp—is, in Sterling Plumpp's words, interested in helping Black students "master as much as we can from these houses of 'miseducation' called schools, colleges, and universities."[5] He is *not* primarily interested in the "academic dress," the "Mercedes," and the "condominiums" ("The New Pimps," p. 57) that the salary of a Black educator can buy. Hence, instead of continually calling attention to himself and his activities (and so quickly being lured away from his Black university and into the Black Studies Department of some White university—where he would, all too often, become little more than a "showcase spade"), the sincere Black educator "very quietly" works at his task of educating his people—usually within the framework of the traditionally Black institution (*Black Rituals*, p. 81).

One might ask just what it is that constitutes "Blackness" in an educator (or in anyone, for that matter). Sterling Plumpp has argued—and argued convincingly—that "Blackness is a state of mind. It is a self-image one has. . . . Blackness is a process of self-discovery, self-assertion, and self-acceptance" (*Black Rituals*, pp. 97-98). Something at least closely akin to Plumpp's definition of Blackness is probably the generally accepted definition of that term among most Black people today. A "Black educator," then, is an educator who has learned, in one way or another, that the prevailing system of education in the United States not only "neglect[s] . . . Afro-American History and distort[s] . . . the facts concerning Negroes in most history books" but it also "deprive[s] the black child and his whole race of a heritage, and relegate[s] him to nothingness and nobodyness." As a result of this awareness, the Black educator not only sometimes openly "criticizes the system"; he also attempts, through his own teaching, to help break "the vicious circle that results from *mis-educated* individuals graduating, then proceeding to teach and *mis-educate* others."[6] And such, I would argue, is the almost religious mission of Black educators like Don L. Lee.

That Lee himself was a victim of the same "mis-education" that Carter G. Woodson and others were concertedly attacking as long ago as 1915[7] was made quite clear in some of the early poetry published by Lee. For example, in an early poem entitled "Education" Lee ironically asserted that:

I had a good teacher,
He taught me everything I know;
how to lie,
    cheat,
    and how to strike the softest blow.
. . . .
My teacher taught me other things too,
. . . how to be inferior without hate.
. . . .
The mistake was made in teaching me
How not to be BLACK.[8]

Finally reacting against this institutionalized mis-education, Lee began the difficult process of self-education. In another of his early poems, "The Self-Hatred of Don L. Lee," Lee describes his difficulty as he struggled to remove the shackles from his mind and to become Black:

after painfully
struggling
thru Du Bois,
Rogers, Locke,
Wright & others,
my blindness
was vanquished
by pitchblack
paragraphs of
"us, we, me, i"
awareness.[9]

Finally, Lee himself made it—

"Back again,
    BLACK AGAIN
        Home."[10]

Unlike the educated pimp (who tends to lose any sense of responsibility to his still-struggling people once he himself has achieved some kind of economic stability), Don Lee did not forget how difficult it had been to remove the shackles from his own mind. Knowing, from personal experience, that "black youth are . . . completely . . . blocked from self-realization in the very institutions that should further it,"[11] Lee determined to dedicate his efforts toward changing the educational system under which Black minds develop in the United States. Moreover, unlike those "educated Negroes" whom Woodson and his coworkers had earlier complained about, Don Lee did not become estranged "from the masses, the very people upon whom [the educator] . . . must eventually count for carrying out a program of progress." He did not ignore "humanity" in the interests of his own "selfishness"; rather, he dedicated himself to what Carter Woodson had earlier called the goal of "developing the masses" and "uplift[ing] . . . a downtrodden people" (*Mis-Education*, pp. 52-56). Like those truly revolutionary educators described by Paulo Freire (a noted Brazilian educator), Lee "join[ed] the oppressed . . . [by] going to them and communicating with them." Don Lee had learned, already, that

"The people must find themselves in the emerging leaders, and the latter must find themselves in the people."[12] There can be no separation of "leaders" from "followers," no imposition of the ideas held by the former upon the latter.

Lee's dedication to—and his continual movement closer to— his people is reflected in all aspects of his teaching career. Having begun his college teaching at Cornell University, a predominantly White institution, Lee soon became disillusioned with what was, apparently, his "showcase spade" role there. That his teaching experiences there were less than completely satisfying to Lee is suggested by his subsequent dedication of *Don't Cry, Scream,* in part, at least, to "my black students at cornell" [sic].[13] Lee's belief that his primary responsibility is to Black students—rather than to White ones—is made clear in this dedication. And it was probably largely this sense of responsibility that soon led him away from the Cornell campus and into the classrooms of Howard University, the so-called "Black Harvard."

Even at Howard, however, Lee has remained a person of movement. Coming to Howard in the fall of 1971 as "Writer-in-Residence," Lee was given a niche in the English department, where he taught one section of a multiple-section course entitled "American Negro Literature." Lee continued to teach this basic literature course for his first three semesters at Howard—although each semester he made significant changes in both the content and the format of the course. Finally, in the spring semester of 1973, Lee moved into the Afro-American Studies department at Howard and began teaching a new literature course that he himself (acting in close conjunction with other potential Black liberators) had designed. The course was entitled, significantly, "Worldview: Toward A New Consciousness." In the course outline that Lee distributed among his students he briefly described the course as follows:

> The major function of this course is to open the students up to the world around them, to give the students other perspectives to work with as they negotiate "their" future. . . . It will provide

a broad study of the historical and contemporary forces that move and motivate man, paying particular attention to the Afri-kan man. . . . In order for this to come about, a great deal of work (Kazi) is necessary. This is to say that much of the reading, research and writing will be completed outside of class. The sessions we spend together will be used for examin-ing and taking apart the material read on the outside.[14]

The "Worldview" course itself is divided into four main problem areas to be discussed during the course of the semester: (1) Definition and Re-Definition, (2) Culture, (3) Biology, Technology, and a Look into the Un-Thought-Of, and (4) The Worldrunners: Who Are They and How Is It Done? Each prob-lem area has been allocated approximately the same amount of class time by Lee, although the "Culture" division is emphasized a little more than is the "Biology, Technology . . ." component of the course. Under each of these problem areas, Lee lists a number of required readings, in addition to citing several other related works that students may wish to consult in the course of their study.[15] Lee also includes in his course outline a brief rationale for these four divisions. The desired ends to be attained from each area of study may be briefly summarized as follows:

1. The first section aims to move students both to an aware-ness of existing prevailing definitions and to a redefinition of themselves and their surroundings.

2. The second section attempts to increase the students' awareness of past Black culture and to stimulate them to con-sider possible ways in which to continue that culture—in mod-ified form—in the future. Special emphasis is given here to the problem of developing/maintaining both a viable Black value system and a Black aesthetic. Students also consider the function of the Black arts within the Black community and the relation-ship of the Black artist to that same community.

3. The third section aims to increase student awareness of certain biological and technological "controls" which influence the lives of Black people today. Confronted by the existence of these "controls," the students will, it is hoped, be stimulated both to learn to understand them more fully and to attempt to

devise some means to react against them/act outside of them. (The importance of increased technological knowledge to the survival of Black people is frequently emphasized by Lee in his teaching; for, like his fellow nationalist, Malaika Jalia, Lee is convinced that "unless . . . [Black people] become proficient in technology we will find that Black folks will end up with the culture and ideology and the white man will still have all of the power.")[16]

4. In the final section the students consider various existing systems of government, giving particular thought to how U.S. foreign policy and foreign affairs relate to the U.S. Black community. Pan-Afrikanism and Afrikan socialism are both considered as possible viable alternatives to the prevailing systems of today.[17]

As can be seen from even this brief description, Lee's "Worldview" course is an extremely ambitious undertaking, requiring much work by both Lee and his students. Even spread over the course of an academic year it would be a challenge for the student; pressed into the confines of a single semester it becomes formidable. As a result, in the semesters that it has been offered, only the most serious students have opted for this course, and the thought/dialogue level in Lee's classroom is generally impressive.

As Don Lee engages in mutual learning/teaching with his students, the *love* of Lee for Black people, the *humility* of Lee himself, and the *faith* that Lee has in *each* person's "power to make and remake, to create and re-create, . . . to be more fully human" are continually apparent. Through relatively nonmanipulated dialogue, Don Lee (teacher/student) and the students/teachers who regularly meet together with him "attempt . . . together, to learn more than they now know" (*Pedagogy,* p. 79). They attempt, together, to determine (1) just what the most pressing problems facing them in today's world are and (2) what different actions might be taken in attempting to solve these problems. Don Lee is obviously well aware that:

since dialogue is the encounter in which the united reflection and action of the dialoguers are addressed to the world which is to be transformed and humanized, this dialogue cannot be reduced to the act of one person's "depositing" ideas in another, nor can it become a simple exchange of ideas to be "consumed" by the discussants. . . . Because dialogue is an encounter among men who name the world, it must not be a situation where some men name on behalf of others. It is an act of creation; it must not serve as a crafty instrument for the domination of one man by another. The domination implicit in dialogue is that of the world by the dialoguers; it is conquest of the world for the liberation of men (*Pedagogy*, p. 77).

Only through nonmanipulated dialogue—conducted in a language that is "attuned to the concrete situation" of the dialoguers —can an intended revolutionary "liberate, and be liberated, with the people" (*Pedagogy*, p. 85; p. 84). And the liberation of himself and his people is the end towards which Don Lee, as Black educator, is moving.

Since at Howard University Lee must operate within the familiar   discrete-time-slot/discrete-subject-matter   substructure that presently informs almost all sectors of the educational establishment in this country, Lee is forced to compromise his educational theories somewhat when he attempts to put them into practice. A system of education like that currently in vogue in the United States seems, in fact, to have been designed primarily for the convenience of administrators rather than for greater learning on the part of students. In fact, practically all U.S. students are, to varying degrees, victims of a rather mind-fragmenting kind of mis-education. The typical college student is required, for example, to concentrate on the principles of human anatomy from 8:00 to 8:50 each Monday, Wednesday, and Friday, then to promptly switch at 9:00 and begin thinking about ancient art, which topic he will in turn dismiss from his mind at 9:50 in order to rearrange his thought patterns for, say, the "distinct subject" called English composition, which he is to "contemplate" until 10:50. This process of "learning," which is repeated daily by most of the students in America, makes it patently impossible for those students to have integrated, nonfragmented minds, minds that are not continually tension-torn.

Such a system of mis-education does, however, make it relatively easy for a student's "progress in/mastery of" any single subject-matter area to be evaluated by the single teacher who discusses that particular subject-matter area with that particular student. The system makes it even easier to maintain student files, academic transcripts, and the like. Expediency, then, seems to be the ultimate *real* goal of the mis-educational system that prevails in this country today.

And within this system Lee is, as I have noted, forced to make certain compromises. These compromises quickly become apparent when one considers a typical class meeting of Lee's "Worldview" course, which runs somewhat as follows: Upon entering the classroom, Lee greets his students with the Swahili greeting, "Habari Gani?" ("What is the news?") With that, the students may respond with "Njema Assante. Habari Gani?" ("Everything is fine, thank you. How's everything with you?") Or, they may begin discussing some item of concern within the Black community—for example, the assassination of Amilcar Cabral, the appearance of Imamu Baraka on campus, or the results of a national election. Perhaps at this time Lee himself will briefly mention some newly released book that relates significantly to the Black liberation struggle. When the discussion flags—or if there is no discussion at this point, Lee will sometimes read a short proverb from Lao-tzu's *The Way of Life*. As a rule, these "sayings" are related both to the current problem under discussion in the classroom and to the larger issue of worldwide Black liberation. After this, Lee often either reads aloud or distributes to each student mimeographed copies of current Black-liberation-related news items that have been gleaned from the daily/weekly papers or from various periodicals—either by some one of the students/teachers or by Lee himself. There follows extended dialogue on the current topic for discussion. At the end of the regular class period, Lee often announces upcoming campus or community events—like lectures, poetry readings, concerts, or art shows. After general exchanges of "Tutaonana Tena" ("We will see one another again"), the majority of the students leave for other classes. Usually, however, a few students remain behind to discuss the current discussion topic at greater length—either with Lee or among themselves.

From this brief description it seems that Lee does, in fact, use a few of those teaching methods that Paulo Freire has so aptly called "banking" techniques, that he does, in part at least, "go to the [people] . . . [attempting] to give them 'knowledge' or to impose upon them the model of the 'good man' contained in a program whose content [he himself has] . . . organized." Such a program, which has, to a certain extent, been "designed . . . according to [the teacher's] . . . own personal view of reality" (*Pedagogy*, pp. 82-83), is, of course, "flawed" from the outset. Nevertheless, in this instance it is "flawed" from necessity, not from design, and, despite its flaws, it is perhaps one of the best *workable* systems of education that is possible in the United States today, given the extremely bureaucratic nature of existing educational institutions.

Several specific "complaints" may be lodged against Lee's method of teaching: (1) each class period is, after all, fairly carefully structured; (2) the use of the Swahili greetings, etc., seems to make the sessions somewhat "elitist"; (3) Lee sometimes seems to be more of a preacher (one who already knows the truth and tells it to others) than he does a revolutionary educator of the type described by Freire (one who learns the truth only with the help of others). One is reminded of Freire's warning/lament about incipient humanist educators/revolutionary leaders (whose end is the simultaneous liberation of themselves and their people):

> Unfortunately . . . in their desire to obtain the support of the people for revolutionary action, revolutionary leaders often fall for the banking line of planning program content from the top down (*Pedagogy*, p. 83).

The rather carefully plotted daily time-structure of Lee's "Worldview" meetings is, however, largely beyond Lee's control, for his course must fit into a larger university-wide schedule of classes—at least as things now stand. Moreover, as indicated above, Lee does frequently continue dialogues after "official" class hours, in an attempt to arrive at possible solutions for certain problems raised in classroom discussion. The structural aspect of the class which most contradicts Lee's teaching theory is more serious than the mere daily time factor. As is apparent from the description given above, the course content itself is largely predetermined by Lee—as opposed to its being arrived at by a general consensus of the dialoguers themselves. While this approach is necessitated by the very nature of the university structure, it also seems to directly contradict both Freire's and Lee's own stated notions about how to choose "the program content of educational . . . action"; such program content must be based upon "the present, existential, concrete situation . . . of the people," and it must "reflect . . . the aspirations of the people" (*Pedagogy*, p. 85)—not the aspirations of the teacher/ student. That the content of Lee's "Worldview" course reflects *only* his own ideas and aspirations is not true, of course; for, as noted above, Lee finally decided upon the content of the course only after extended dialogue with many other Black teachers/students and students/teachers. Considering that Lee sees *all* Black people as part of one worldwide "extended family," he did, then, in effect, take "into account . . . the *men-in-a-situation* to whom [his] . . . program was . . . directed" (*Pedagogy*, p. 83). Moreover, the problem of imposing predetermined course content upon his students will surely be difficult for Lee to solve completely—for at Howard each academic term is only approximately twelve weeks long, and a teacher does not know exactly who will be dialoguing with him until the first day of class.

Such "advance planning" of course content by the teacher seems to be unavoidable. Perhaps, however, if preregistration occurred earlier and if printed class lists were given to instructors several months in advance, teachers could meet in advance with students to determine what problems should be considered in their upcoming courses. Until such happens, it seems almost impossible for an educator to avoid, at least to some extent, speaking "to the people about [his] . . . own view of the world" and attempting "to impose that view on them" (*Pedagogy*, p.

85). The dialogue portion (the major portion) of each class period is, even now, unstructured; that is, Lee does not have some predetermined conclusion towards which the class is subtly being directed (by Lee) during the dialogue. Frequently Lee, in his role as teacher/student, seems to learn nearly as much from the dialogue as his assembled students/teachers do.

Although Lee does both greet and say farewell to the class in Swahili, he does not do this in order to foster elitist sentiment within the group. On the contrary, the Swahili expressions are intended to engender a greater sense of group (i.e., Pan-Afrikan) commitment within each dialoguer, by reminding him that he is indeed an Afrikan and, as such, he is "brother" to other Afrikans throughout the diaspora. By encouraging his students to begin to learn Swahili "with its collective nuances rather than individualistic directive," Lee is almost surely hoping to help bring about each student's realization of "the importance of the co-operative nature of man over the individualistic."[18]

The almost religious nature of Lee's educational methods should also be clear from the preceding description of his classroom techniques. In fact, participating in a typical class meeting is, in many ways, almost like attending a church service. If Lee might be envisioned as a kind of "preacher," then his opening greeting (in Swahili) might be seen as the equivalent of an invocation, while his closing farewell could be considered a kind of benediction. Similarly, his brief proverb from Lao-tzu, due to its usually close relationship to the topic under discussion, serves almost the same purpose as a preacher's scriptural text for the day: just as the scriptural text epitomizes the larger sermon, so Lee's proverb usually embodies/sheds light on the problem to be confronted. Moreover, just as a preacher's ultimate goal is to liberate his "flock" from "the sins of the flesh" and to move them into a kind of "new world," so Lee's goal is to liberate himself and his fellow dialoguers from both mental and physical oppression so that each can become a fully conscious shaper of a new Black Nation. There is one major difference between Don Lee and a preacher, however: a preacher already *knows* "the truth" about reality and, elevated slightly above his parishioners (both physically, at the pulpit, and mentally, in his own mind), he attempts to "deposit" within his listening—and silent—parishioners some knowledge of that (unchanging) reality. Lee, who either sits at a table or stands at a lectern which is on the same level as the desks of his students/ teachers, depends upon the critical thinking of his fellow dialoguers to enable them all both to understand and to creatively transform an ever-changing reality. What might be called the "religious overtones" of Lee's teaching practice are surely not merely chance phenomena, however; for Lee, like the earlier Black liberationist Marcus Garvey, is "well acquainted with the tremendous influence of religion in the life of the Negro." And, like Garvey, Lee seems to be consciously attempting to "assimilat[e] . . . the religious experience of the Negro . . . [into] his own program."[19]

That Lee is above all dedicated to his people, rather than to himself (i.e., his own individual materialistic success) and that he does, indeed, see himself as a liberator of/with his people are reflected in Lee's *manner*, as well as in his *method*, in the classroom. He is at once quietly soft-spoken and intensely sincere; his "academic attire" is at once perfectly practical, extremely neat, and, as a rule, rather outdated. Lee's concerns—like those of his most attentive dialoguers—are far more weighty than the "problem" of staying in tune with the latest fashions. As Lee himself has often remarked, a "worldrunner" has far more serious things to concern himself with than the cuff-width of his bell-bottomed trousers! Dressing, speaking, and thinking as one with the people, Lee himself suffers from no elitist "delusions of grandeur." And it is probably largely this sincerity— in conjunction with Lee's completely unassuming manner—that attracts various Howard University students to Lee's classroom and keeps them there—in spite of the large amount of work expected of them by Lee. There is a kind of *honesty* in Lee's classroom that is, as Paulo Freire has repeatedly emphasized, essential to the learning process. There is also a strong—and shared—feeling of mutual respect and love among Lee, teacher/ student, and his students/teachers, which reinforces the feeling of "Ujamaa" or "familyhood" that prevails in Lee's classroom as the assembled dialoguers actively engage in their quest for mutual liberation.

The educational activities of Don Lee are *not*, however, confined to the Howard classrooms—or even to the Howard University campus. Lee maintains strong ties with the larger Black communities of both Washington, D.C. and Chicago. In both of these areas, Lee makes frequent speaking appearances at the local Black schools (speaking to students of all age levels), where he reads his poetry and talks to the students about the need for a viable Black value system.[20] Lee also "teaches" in this manner at community centers, in parks, and at bookstores —not only in the Washington and Chicago Black communities, but elsewhere, as his time permits. Moreover, Lee frequently, and effectively, teaches Black cultural values through the medium of the Black press[21] and, in his additional roles as publisher /editor of Third World Press, executive director of the Institute of Positive Education, and editor of the *Black Books Bulletin*, Lee helps to infuse into Black communities throughout this country an accumulation of what is probably some of the best of contemporary Black thought.

Believing, as did Carter G. Woodson before him, that the youth of a nation are the ones most in need of proper education, Lee concentrates much of his effort on youth-education projects. Probably his most successful venture into this area is his involvement with the New Concept School, a Black community school in Chicago.[22] Despite his emphasis on youth-training, however, Lee has not completely abandoned older Black students/teachers (or even teachers/students); for older people are present at, and participate in, most of his community-wide educational projects, and Lee is a fairly regular speaker on the educator-convention circuit.

The extent, the diversity, and the quality of Lee's educational activities suggest many parallels between Lee's career as a Black educator and the similarly multi-faceted career of an earlier Black educator, Carter Woodson. Like Lee, Woodson was, for some time, a faculty member at Howard University; and, in addition to doing classroom teaching and extra-classroom lecturing, Woodson also wrote numerous articles and books, which were meant to help correct many of the false notions that Black youth were receiving in the mis-educational institutions of the United States in the early decades of this century. Woodson also helped to found the Association for the Study of Negro Life and History, which organization was—and still is, although perhaps to a lesser degree—noted for its "Black nationalistic" activities and goals. Moreover, Woodson helped to establish and edit the *Journal of Negro History,* a vehicle in which were published the works of like-minded scholars. Again like Lee, Woodson was "convinced of the interrelations of all types of social phenomena," so he encouraged Black educators to teach social customs, literature, economic and political materials—to teach everything, in fact, that might affect the lives of Black students (*Mis-Education,* p. xvii). The existence of so many parallels in the careers of these two Black educators suggests that Lee may be consciously modeling himself, as Black educator, at least in part after the early example of Woodson. Such striking parallels may, however, merely result from the fact that Lee does, as did Woodson, firmly believe that educational programs should be non-rigid, very flexible, and constantly changing—in order to equip students with the necessary skills not just to survive but to thrive in a constantly changing world.[23]

Perhaps even more striking similarities become apparent when one considers the career of Don Lee, Black educator/liberator in light of the career of an early Afrikan reformer/revolutionary, Shehu ("teacher/savior") Usuman Dan Fodio. Like both Woodson and Lee, Dan Fodio, a late-eighteenth/early-nineteenth-century Hausa teacher/preacher in the Sudan, had a center of teaching (the city of Degel), but he travelled widely, teaching—and living—his ideas and ideals. Because in his own lifestyle he embodied those principles that he taught, Dan Fodio attracted to himself large groups of devoted Hausa followers. Moreover, in addition to his teaching, Dan Fodio was a prolific writer, and

> many of the books Dan Fodio wrote were intended to be text-books for the many schools spread all over Hausaland which looked to Degel [Dan Fodio's "headquarters"] for guidance and direction. Dan Fodio used to recommend certain books to be given priority in teaching. He kept in touch with his old pupils by compiling short works as teacher's handbooks—to give advice.[24]

Having built up, through these varied means, an ideologically closeknit—but geographically widespread—cadre of followers who adhered to similar beliefs, Dan Fodio moved, in the closing years of the eighteenth century, to lead his followers in a *Jihād* (a kind of religious war)—the immediate goal of which was to initiate widespread religious reforms in Hausaland but whose secondary goal was to effect needed changes at *all* levels of Islamic life (religious, political, social, domestic, and even in the private lives of Muslims), both within Hausaland and beyond. Because of Dan Fodio's years of steady teaching and exemplary living, large numbers of his former students rallied to support him, and "Shehu Usuman dan Fodio through his force of character, piety, preaching, his pupils and books led a successful *Jihād*."[25]

As was pointed out earlier, there are many religious overtones in Lee's methodology as a teacher. There is, moreover, an intense feeling of camaraderie—almost discipleship—among Lee's "Worldview" students. The cadre-spirit that permeates Lee's classroom also spills over into the lives of his students outside the classroom. Many of Lee's most serious dialoguers have begun implementing different facets of the various "alternate lifestyles" that are discussed in Lee's classroom. Such external changes as clothing, diet, and cooperative purchasing/cooking/studying/tutoring ventures provide visible evidence of certain definite changes which are taking place in Lee's dialoguers, as they move from what Edward De Bono has called "vertical thinking" into the more positive habit of "lateral thinking."[26] Probably the most significant changes, however, are those ideological ones that occur as each student/teacher attempts to understand how the world operates and tries to define both himself and his relationship to the larger world.

Lee's ability to inspire almost religious devotion in his closest followers[27] has been recognized by many other incipient Black liberators. In fact, when speaking of the "liberating" quality of Lee's poetry, Sterling Plumpp goes so far as to argue that

> the terms of his art are such that Black people respond to it the way they respond to down home revivals. Don L. Lee is really an old-time preacher using the street symbols, corner raps and the Black Position as his bibles; when he reads his poetry, he preaches, he teaches, he condemns, he lauds, he instills hope, and he warns of damnation. The problem the Black man faces today is for Don L. Lee to get a church and to carry on in the tradition of a Bishop Turner.[28]

Because Plumpp believes, basically, that (1) the Black church is the only Black institution that is really controlled by Black people and (2) it was the past failure of the Black church to meet the needs of Black people that caused the Black man's plight today, he is, in essence, arguing that only through a re-infusion of Black nationalistic spirit into the Black church (through people/preachers like Don L. Lee) can Black people in the United States be effectively "reborn" or "recreated."

Don Lee, however, in choosing to operate from a Black classroom's podium, rather than from a Black church's pulpit, reflects his belief that Black liberation can, in fact, be effected by working through yet a second Black institution: the traditionally Black school. Like many other Black educators today, Lee seems to believe that

> the major community contribution of the black college will be the training of secure leadership that will assume responsibility for engineering social change.[29]

To help insure that future Black leaders will be "secure," Lee, in his classroom teaching, actively works *against* what Plumpp has called "the Ritual of Fathers," according to which "only one [Black person] . . . at a time can have a will, and need to use it" (*Black Rituals*, p. 57). That is, as indicated earlier, Lee discourages his students/teachers from believing that he alone knows "the truth" about any problem or solution. All persons in the room are seekers after the truth and, working together, they often discover at least a part of it. Hence, when it occasionally happens that Lee cannot be present at a scheduled class meeting, the class is not dismissed; rather, one of Lee's students/teachers will propose some "problem," and the dialogue will continue.

Lee's essentially egalitarian teaching method is, in the final analysis, an extremely *practical* one. Although past Black leaders as different as Nat Turner, Malcolm X, and Martin Luther King have used the "messianic" approach to build a large following, there are inherent flaws in this method. If the leader of a movement has allowed himself to become, in effect, "The One" (that is, the *only* one who has complete access to the truth and can, consequently, "deposit" that truth in the minds of his followers) and if that leader is then killed—as were Nat Turner, Malcolm X, and Martin Luther King—in the heyday of his movement, both the movement and the followers themselves tend to "fall apart"—at least temporarily—and considerable ground is usually lost, in terms of achieving the goals of that movement. Divided leadership, then, makes for greater strength in a movement.

Lee, who is concerned more with the liberation both of himself and his fellow Black people than he is with becoming the object of mass adulation, chooses a slightly different route from that of other present-day potential Black liberators like, say, Imamu Amiri Baraka. Baraka, although almost surely as deeply concerned with effecting the liberation of his people as is Don Lee, goes about the struggle in what seems, at times, to be an almost self-defeating manner. For example, publicly doffing his "slavery given name," Baraka (formerly "LeRoi Jones") adopted a rather openly challenging name; thus, "LeRoi Jones" became "Imamu Amiri Baraka"—which translates, roughly, to mean "Prayer Leader/Prince/Man with Spiritual Powers." As an even more open challenge, Baraka established his Jihād Publishing Company in "New Ark." While these symbolic "labels" did serve as effective rallying points for Black people, they also announced that Baraka, an emerging Black leader, presented almost a "clear and present danger" to the White Establishment in this country, and Baraka not only was closely watched but was harassed by the Establishment. Although he was "important" enough, in the eyes of Establishment leaders, to have had a "hotline to Anthony Imperiale's North Ward Citizens Council after the 1967 Newark riots," he probably got a wiretap along with it—if he didn't have one already! Moreover Baraka, currently the prime mover behind "Kawaida Towers, a [planned] high-rise apartment building for [Black] low- and middle-income families in a hitherto predominantly white area" of Newark,[30] finds his plans being thwarted at every turn.

There is something to be said for open challenges: they are honest and, often, noble. But, too often those who have openly thrown down the gauntlet before the entrenched Establishment turn up dead (Malcolm X, Martin Luther King), or jailed (Maulana Ron Karenga, Angela Davis), or exiled (Stokely Carmichael, Eldridge Cleaver). At best, such overtly challenging leaders as Baraka, by succumbing to what Sterling Plumpp has called "psychological oligarchism" (*Black Rituals*, p. 58), and adopting names that effectively set them apart from the mass of Black people, are narrowing their base of support among the people. For, when confronted by an "Imamu" or a "Maulana" ("Spiritual Leader"), an "ordinary" Black person will tend both to be awed and to feel somewhat insignificant. And such feelings on the part of the Black masses clearly do not strengthen the Black "liberation front" in this country. Revolutionaries like Baraka might do well to remember Julius Nyerere's warning, given in 1966, that "Leaders must not be Masters"; rather:

When you are selected to lead your fellow men, it does not mean that you know everything better than they do. It does not

even mean that you are more intelligent than they are—especially
the elders. . . . [The] aim [of leaders] is to hand over responsibility to the people to make their own decisions. Our leaders . . .
are elected by the people. . . . Our leaders must be chosen by
us.[31]

When the elements of fear and awe enter the people's minds
as they regard their leader, the effectiveness of that leader becomes severely limited. Meanwhile, those who oppose the status
quo more quietly and unobtrusively are still at work—in the
public library, at the health-food store, at the precinct meeting
place, in their cooperative business establishments, in their
laboratories, or perhaps even in the classroom. They are, as
Lee himself has said of his fellow Black revolutionary, Charlie
Cobb, "now somewhere working quietly for [their] people."[32]

"Quiet workers" like Don Lee, who elect to base their liberation activities within the traditionally "conservative" Black
school system, have, then, several advantages over highly visible
—and more highly "political" (in the conventional sense)—potential liberators like Baraka. Because of the curious anti-intel-
lectual bias that has prevailed in this country almost from its
founding, educators—of whatever color—are generally regarded
as "harmless drudges," "eggheads," and the like. Consequently,
they—and their activities—are largely ignored. The same is not
true of political/civic leaders, however. For almost everyone
has heard the old adage that "To be a politician, one must be
at least *a little bit* corrupt!" Hence, politicians, particularly in
this "Era of Watergate," are to be feared—and *watched*. In a
like manner, most Americans firmly believe that Black people are
inherently an intensely religious people—so religious, in fact,
that almost any leader who is going to amass a large following
must inevitably come from within the ranks of Black church
leadership. Hence, Black religious leaders are also closely
watched by the predominantly White Establishment. Simply by
choosing to work from within the educational system, then, Lee
has gained an advantage. By choosing to operate from within
the traditionally Black school system, Lee has gained an even

greater advantage. If educators as a whole tend to be ignored in the United States, Black educators are almost surely among the most ignored. The relatively greater "insignificance" of the Black educator, in the eyes of the predominantly White Establishment, stems, of course, from "the negative biases of [the] white public . . . about [Black] . . . schools—and more generally about black people"[33]—in short, from entrenched racism.

The Black school has several additional built-in advantages as a staging ground for the Black liberation movement. Even extremely small Black communities often contain several churches (of different denominations). This multiplicity of churches would, of necessity, create divided loyalties within citizens of the community—if any *one* church were chosen by the liberation leader as his "headquarters." If *all* the churches within such multiple-denominational communities were used as vehicles for liberation, there would—in the beginning, at least—not be enough trained leaders. For present preachers would almost invariably need to be re-educated themselves—towards community service. Even middle-sized Black communities, however, usually have only one educational system, and, considering the recent nationwide trend towards more and more local control of schools, the Black communities of this nation presently have more actual control over their educational systems than at any other time in U.S. history. Moreover, because of the legal requirement of compulsory education for all children, all Black children between the ages of approximately six and sixteen are legally *required*, barring illness and the like, to be present in schools for approximately seven hours a day, five days a week, thirty-six weeks a year. *No* Black child is *required* to attend church for thirty-five hours each week. Those who attend at all do so voluntarily, and they are seldom present in church for as much as seven hours weekly (one day's required attendance time at school!). It would be incredibly shortsighted for potential Black liberators to ignore this ready-made opportunity for influencing /shaping Black children's minds.

No matter what the economic status of a Black community,

the physical plant of the local school is usually both bigger and better than that of any single area church. Local school systems also have special equipment that is not found in most churches: typewriters and other business machines, machine-shop equipment, library books, "practice kitchens" in home economics departments, assorted sports equipment, musical instruments, science laboratories, cafeteria/lunchroom equipment. Some large high schools even have computers. All of these things could readily be adapted for use in the Black liberation struggle.

If community schools really were to become "centers for community learning," music and art departments might institute biweekly "Black Culture Nights"; physical education departments might organize weekly family recreation/exercise nights; home economics departments might sponsor biweekly community ("potluck") dinners. Journalism or English departments might contrive to establish and run small community-centered newspapers. Saturdays might be devoted to literary discussion groups led by members of the school's library staff. The agriculture department might institute weekly cooperative exchange markets —where students and other residents of the community could exchange crops and livestock—as well as information on new and better farming techniques. There might be Saturday instruction for both men and women in the basics of auto mechanics. Students of business and economics might organize discussion groups for people interested in learning the basics of intelligent consumerism. Young scientists could use lab equipment to study possible cures for animal and plant diseases indigenous to their area. The possibilities for meaningful school/community interaction are almost limitless.

Valuable community functions might also be fulfilled by the Black colleges—particularly those colleges that maintain cooperative education programs. When cooperative education students (who usually alternate their semesters between on-campus study and off-campus employment) left the campus for their "work semesters," they could go into Black communities throughout this country to work. Those student-workers with expertise in journalism or communications could work in Black-oriented media systems: the press, radio, television, advertising. Students in the field of business could work with businessmen in the Black community who were committed to Black survival and advancement. Those who were enrolled in teacher-training programs could progress from being "teachers' aides" to doing their student-teaching in Black community schools. Medical and dental students could work in health clinics and hospitals that serve mostly a Black clientele. Youthful engineers and architects could work with their older (established) community counterparts to design and build much-needed housing units, hospitals, shopping centers, office buildings, transportation facilities, and the like for the large urban Black communities of America. Moreover, students of law, if subsidized by a "community legal fund," could combine to provide legal aid for poor families at no—or at minimal—cost.

Such a positive contribution to community progress on the part of Black schools—at all levels—would inevitably lead to a resurgence of community interest in schools within Black communities everywhere. From this new interest would almost surely develop, in time, broad programs like continuing ("adult") education, preschool instruction, and day-care facilities for the preschool children of working parents. Moreover, if people within a community could see how their tax monies "for education" were actually being spent and if they themselves—even though they had no school-age children—were reaping some direct benefits from those tax dollars, they would be far more inclined to raise their own taxes when the need for increased tax monies occurred. Schools clearly *can*, then, become a major cohesive force within the Black community.

Don Lee and other Black educators of his type clearly understand both that White Establishment which they are attempting to undermine and that Black community which they are attempting to advance. Knowing Establishment weaknesses, they use them to their own advantage. Knowing the strengths of the Black community, they do likewise. The final goal of such Black

educators is, as indicated above, the liberation of themselves and
their people. They desire that each man should have both mental and physical control over his own destiny—that he should be,
in effect, the shaper of his own life. Working together, through
already established, and traditionally Black, educational institutions, such Black educators as Lee attempt to awaken in Black
students/teachers an awareness

> of the black predicament [in today's world] and [to] pro-
> vid[e] . . . for serious discussion of the goals, both long and
> short term, of black people and of the most expeditious means
> for their realization. . . . From this new perspective a sustaining
> ideology would automatically flower, an ideology that would ac-
> centuate peoplehood among Africans throughout the diaspora. It
> would define both their allies and enemies, order their priorities,
> and etch in the contours of the future they envision for their
> progeny.[34]

Thus, such Black educators as Lee work quietly to insure that
Black educational institutions in the United States become
meaningful instruments for positive change—as, for example,
the schools in Tanzania are becoming under the leadership of
President Nyerere and the schools in China have become under
Chairman Mao.

In the United States, as in these other countries, "The question of educational reform is mainly a question of teachers."[35]
It is hoped that, through reading about the teaching methods
of Don Lee, a relatively successful Black educator, other struggling Black educators not only will be encouraged to continue
their struggle against the rather firmly entrenched system of
mis-education that prevails in the United States but will perhaps learn some useful (and adaptable) teaching techniques.[36]
Such a sharing of knowledge is extremely important; for, as
President Julius K. Nyerere of Tanzania declared in a 1966
speech dealing with "The Power of Teachers":

> Teachers can make or ruin our society. As a group they have a
> power which is second to none. It is not the power of a man
> with a gun; it is not a power which can be seen by the fool. . . .

The [actual] power of teachers is not the less [however] because it is usually unacknowledged.

On the contrary, education—or mis-education—can be even "'more deadly . . . [than] massacre . . . in the long run.' "[37]

NOTES

1. See Lee's essay entitled "Where Are the Black Educators Who Are Educated Blackly?" *From Plan to Planet, Life Studies: The Need for Afrikan Minds and Institutions* (Detroit: Broadside Press, 1973), pp. 35-41.

2. Cheek's strong stand in support of Black Studies has received fairly broad coverage in the nation's press. See, for example, "Debate Flares on Merit of Black Studies in Negro College," which appeared (under a *Washington Post* Service byline) as far away as *The Arizona Republic*, Jan. 18, 1973, p. C8. Also see Alex Poinsett, "The Metamorphosis of Howard University," *Ebony*, XXVII (Dec., 1971), 110-112; 114; 116; 118; 120; 122.

3. I myself have rather carefully observed Lee's classroom teaching methods—for, as a post-doctoral student, I audited both Lee's "American Negro Literature" course in the fall semester of 1972-1973 and his course entitled "Worldview: Toward a New Consciousness" in the spring semester of that same academic year.

4. See Lee's essay, "The New Pimps/ or it's Hip to be Black: the Failure of Black Studies," *From Plan to Planet*, pp. 55-61.

5. Sterling D. Plumpp, *Black Rituals* (Chicago: Third World Press, 1972), p. 81.

6. See Carter Godwin Woodson, *The Mis-Education of the Negro*, reissue (Washington, D. C.: The Association Publishers, Inc., 1969), pp. vi-vii—hereafter referred to as *Mis-Education*.

7. Woodson and four other Black educators combined to found the Association for the Study of Negro Life and History in 1915, and the Association began publishing its quarterly, *The Journal of Negro History*, in 1916.

8. *Think Black!* 3rd (enlarged) ed. (Detroit: Broadside Press, 1969), p. 11.

9. *Black Pride* (Detroit: Broadside Press, 1968), p. 19.

10. See "Back Again, Home," *Think Black!* p. 7.

11. See Chancellor Williams, *The Destruction of Black Civilization: Great Issues of a Race from 4500 B.C. to 2000 A.D.* (Dubuque, Iowa: Kendall/Hunt Pub. Co., 1971), p. xix.

12. Paulo Freire, *Pedagogy of the Oppressed,* trans. Myra Berg-

man Ramos (New York, 1972), p. 162—hereafter referred to as *Pedagogy.*

13. *Don't Cry, Scream* (Detroit: Broadside Press, 1969), p. 5. For further insight into Lee's Cornell experiences, see David Llorens, "Black Don Lee," *Ebony,* XXIV (March, 1969), 72-78; 80.

14. This course description is an amalgam of Lee's own statements which appeared on various handouts distributed by Lee in his "Worldview" classroom in the spring semester of 1972-1973.

15. With Don Lee's permission, I have included as Appendix A to this book a list containing both the *required* readings and the *suggested* readings for Lee's spring semester, 1972-1973, "Worldview" course. (Lee also provides each of his students with a supplemental "Functional Reading List," which list is regularly updated by Lee. A 1972 version of this "Functional Reading List" appears on pp. 149-158 of *From Plan to Planet.*)

16. See Jalia's "The Importance of Technology to Black People," in *African Congress: A Documentary of the First Modern Pan-African Congress,* ed. Imamu Amiri Baraka (New York: William Morrow, 1972), pp. 235-239; quotation appears on p. 238.

17. Again, this description of both the divisions and the "ends" of Lee's course is taken largely from various handouts distributed by Lee in his "Worldview" classroom in the spring semester of 1972-1973. The many similarities between Lee's "Worldview" course and the Black Studies curriculum proposed by Maulana Ron Karenga at the spring 1968 conference of professional educators held at Yale University become readily apparent when one considers Lee's course in light of Karenga's comments at that conference. These comments appear in "The Black Community and the University: A Community Organizer's Perspective," *Black Studies in the University: A Symposium,* ed. Armstead L. Robinson, Craig C. Foster, and Donald H. Ogilvie (New York: Yale Univ. Press, 1969), pp. 38-56.

18. See Lee's essay, "Communications: The Language of Control," *From Plan to Planet,* p. 51.

19. For an excellent discussion of Garvey's use of various religious rituals in his back-to-Afrika movement of the 1920s, see E. Franklin Frazier, "Garvey: A Mass Leader," in *The Black Man and the American Dream: Negro Aspirations in America, 1900-1930,* ed. June Sochen (Chicago: Quadrangle Books, Inc., 1971), pp. 331-335. The quoted material appears on p. 334.

20. Many of Lee's main ideas concerning a Black value system are quite similar to those tenets espoused by Imamu Amiri Baraka (LeRoi Jones) in *Kawaida Studies: The New Nationalism* (Chicago: Third World Press, 1972).

21. See, for example, "Don L. Lee Teaching Cultural Values," *Third World*, Nov. 3, 1972, p. 1; p. 11.

22. For information about and illustrations of the New Concept School (as well as for further information concerning Lee's educational theories), see *From Plan to Planet*, pp. 64-74. For information regarding a similar Black community school in Newark, The African Free School (where Lee's fellow Black Nation builder, Imamu Baraka, is involved in the education of Black youths), see Baraka's "Black Woman," in *Kawaida Studies: The New Nationalism*.

23. For further information concerning both the career and the probable influence of Carter G. Woodson, consult both the introduction and the preface to *The Mis-Education of the Negro*, pp. v-xxxiv.

24. F. H. El-Masri, "The Life of Shehu Usuman Dan Fodio Before the Jihād," *JHSN, II* (Dec., 1963), 443.

25. El-Masri, 447.

26. See Edward De Bono, *New Think: The Use of Lateral Thinking in the Generation of New Ideas* (New York: Avon Books, 1971).

27. For an excellent fictionalized account of just how this tendency of Black people to almost deify their leaders ultimately affects both those leaders and the Black (and White) communities in which they function, see Book IV ("The Quarters") of Ernest J. Gaines, *The Autobiography of Miss Jane Pittman*, Bantam paperback ed. (New York, 1972), pp. 199-246.

28. *Black Rituals*, p. 99. Bishop Henry M. Turner, of the African Methodist Episcopal Church in Georgia, was a powerful post-Reconstruction Black nationalist who used the church as a vehicle for social reform.

29. See Patricia Roberts Harris, "The Negro College and Its Community," *Daedalus,* Vol. 100 (Summer, 1971), 729. (This entire volume of *Daedalus* is concerned with "The Future of the Black Colleges.")

30. See Ross K. Baker, "Black Nationalism on the Upswing," *The Washington Post*, Jan. 28, 1973, p. B2, col. 4; col. 3.

31. Julius K. Nyerere, *Freedom and Socialism/Uhuru na Ujamaa: A Selection from Writings and Speeches 1965-1967* (New York: Oxford University Press, 1968), p. 140.

32. See the note on the back cover of Charlie Cobb's *Everywhere Is Yours* (Chicago: Third World Press, 1971).

33. Tobe Johnson, "The Black College as System," *Daedalus,* 798. (See above, note 29.)

34. Mack H. Jones, "The Responsibility of the Black College to the Black Community: Then and Now," *Daedalus,* 740-741. (See above, note 29.)

35. See "How the Young Are Taught in Mao's China," *SR* (March 4, 1972), p. 44.

36. Courses similar to "Worldview" would, it seems, offer broad opportunities for interdisciplinary, team-teaching experiments.

37. Nyerere's speech was given on August 27, 1966, at the opening ceremonies of the Morogoro Teachers' College, located 120 miles from Dar es Salaam. This speech is reprinted in *Freedom and Socialism/Uhuru na Ujamaa*, pp. 223-228. See p. 228 for quoted material —part of which represents Nyerere quoting Mark Twain on the power of education.

A Selected Bibliography
of Published Works
by and about Don L. Lee

BY DON L. LEE

Books and Pamphlets

Brown, Patricia L., Don L. Lee, and Francis Ward, eds. *To Gwen with Love: An Anthology Dedicated to Gwendolyn Brooks*. Chicago: Johnson Pub. Co., 1971.

Lee, Don L. *Black Pride*. Detroit: Broadside Press, 1968.

_____. *Directionscore: Selected and New Poems*. Detroit: Broadside Press, 1971.

_____. *Don't Cry, Scream*. Detroit: Broadside Press, 1969.

_____. *Dynamite Voices I: Black Poets of the 1960's*. Detroit: Broadside Press, 1971.

_____. *Europe and Africa: A Poet's View—Part I*. Chicago: IPE, 1972.

_____. *From Plan to Planet, Life Studies: The Need for Afrikan Minds and Institutions*. Detroit: Broadside Press, 1973.

_____. *Think Black!* Chicago: Nu-Ace Social Printers, 1967.

_____. *Think Black!* 3rd (enlarged) ed. Detroit: Broadside Press, 1969.

_____. *We Walk the Way of the New World*. Detroit: Broadside Press, 1970.

Articles

Lee, Don L. "Black Poetry: Which Direction?" *Negro Digest*
XVII (Sept.-Oct., 1968): 27-32.
————. "The Black Writer and the Black Community." *Black
World* XXI (May, 1972): 85-87.
————. "Black Writers' Views on Literary Lions and Values."
Negro Digest XVII (Jan., 1968): 44; 89.
————. "Communications: The Language of Control." *The
Black Position* No. 2 (1972): 43-47.
————. "Directions for Black Writers." *The Black Scholar*
I (Dec., 1969): 53-57.
————. "Don L. Lee Interviews Stokely Carmichael." *Journal
of Black Poetry* I (Special Pan-African Issue, 1970-1971):
70-81.
————. "Don L. Lee Teaching Cultural Values." *Third World*,
Nov. 3, 1972, p. 1; p. 11.
————. "Dynamite Voices: Black Poets of the 1970's." *African
Congress: A Documentary of the First Modern Pan-African
Congress.* Ed. Imamu Amiri Baraka (LeRoi Jones). New
York: William Morrow & Company, 1972, pp. 200-211.
————. "If I Call U Negro, You'll Act That Way!" *Black
World* XIX (Oct., 1970): 44-45.
————. "The Measure and Meaning of the Sixties: What Lies
Ahead for Black Americans?" *Negro Digest* XIX (Nov.,
1969): 11-14.
————. "The Need for an Afrikan Education." *The Black
Collegian* III (Jan.-Feb., 1973): 23-24.
————. "The New Pimps or, It's Hip to be Black: The Failure
of Black Studies." *The Black Position* No. 1 (1971): 9-11.
————. "Notes from a Black Journal." *Negro Digest* XIX
(Jan., 1970): 11; 85-89.
————. "Statement . . . 'Black Poetics/for the many to come.'"
NOMMO: The Journal of the OBAC Writers' Workshop
I (Summer, 1972): 30.
————. "Tomorrow Is Tomorrow If You Want One." *The*

Black Seventies. Ed. Floyd B. Barbour. Boston: Sargent, Porter, Pub., 1970, pp. 241-251.

_____. "Toward a Definition: Black Poetry of the Sixties (After LeRoi Jones)." *The Black Aesthetic.* Ed. Addison Gayle, Jr. New York: Doubleday & Company, 1972, pp. 222-233.

_____. "Voices of the Seventies: Black Critics." *Black World* XIX (Sept., 1970): 24-30.

_____. "What We Are About." *Black Books Bulletin* I (Fall, 1971): 25.

_____. "Worldview." *Black Books Bulletin* I (Winter, 1972): 11.

_____. "Worldview: Europe and Africa." *Black Books Bulletin* I (Spring-Summer): 49-51.

Lee, Don L. and Plumpp, Sterling. "Editorial." *Black Books Bulletin* I (Spring-Summer, 1972): 42.

Introductions, Afterwords, and Book Reviews

Lee, Don L. Afterword. *To Gwen with Love: An Anthology Dedicated to Gwendolyn Brooks.* Eds. Patricia L. Brown, Don L. Lee, and Francis Ward. Chicago: Johnson Pub. Co., 1971, p. 135.

_____. "Black Writing: this is u, thisisu." *Negro Digest* XVIII (March, 1969): 51-52; 78-81. (Review of LeRoi Jones's *Black Fire.)*

_____. "Gwendolyn Brooks: Beyond the Wordmaker—The Making of an African Poet." Preface to Gwendolyn Brooks's *Report from Part One.* Detroit: Broadside Press, 1972, pp. 13-30.

_____. Introduction to Sonia Sanchez's *Home Coming.* Detroit: Broadside Press, 1969, pp. 6-8.

_____. Introduction. *WATU: Journal of Black Poetry/Art,* I (Cornell University, 1969).

_____. "The Man Who Cried I Am." *Negro Digest* XVII (March, 1968): 51-52; 77-79.

_____. "Needed: A Native Son to Write About a Native

Son." *Negro Digest* XVII (July, 1968): 85-88. (Review of Constance Webb's biography, *Richard Wright.*)

_____. "On *Kaleidoscope* and Robert Hayden." *Negro Digest* XVII (Jan., 1968): 51-52; 90-94.

_____. ["The Still Voice of Harlem"]. *Negro Digest* XVII (Aug., 1968): 94-97.

_____. "The Way of the Black Word." Introduction to Norman Jordan's *Destination: Ashes.* Chicago: Third World Press, 1970, pp. 13-16.

_____. "Why This Issue?" *Journal of Black Poetry* I (Special Pan-African Issue, 1970-1971): 2-3.

_____. "A Word." *NOMMO: The Journal of the OBAC Writers' Workshop* I (Summer, 1972): 32.

_____. "Words in the Early Time: An Introduction." *Black Spirits: A Festival of New Black Poets in America.* Ed. Woodie King. New York: Random House, Inc., 1972, pp. xvii-xxviii.

Broadsides

Lee, Don L. "Assassination." Broadside No. 25. Detroit: Broadside Press.

_____. "Back Again, Home." Broadside No. 16. Detroit: Broadside Press.

_____. "For Black People and Negroes." Chicago: Third World Press, 1968.

_____. "One-Sided Shoot-Out." Broadside No. 33. Detroit: Broadside Press.

Anthologies Containing Lee's Work

Adoff, Arnold, ed. *Black Out Loud: An Anthology of Modern Poems by Black Americans.* New York: Macmillan Publishing Co., 1970, p. 2; p. 29; p. 56.

_____. *City in All Directions: An Anthology of Modern Poems.* New York: Macmillan Publishing Co., 1969, p. 30.

Alhamisi, Ahmed and Wangara, Harun Kofi, eds. *Black Arts:*

An Anthology of Black Creations. Detroit: Black Arts Publications, 1969, pp. 95-98.

Baker, Houston A., Jr., ed. *Black Literature in America*. New York: McGraw-Hill Book Co., 1971, pp. 419-422.

Barksdale, Richard and Kinnamon, Keneth, eds. *Black Writers of America: A Comprehensive Anthology*. New York: Macmillan Publishing Co., 1972, pp. 821-822.

Bell, Bernard W., ed. *Modern and Contemporary Afro-American Poetry*. Boston: Allyn & Bacon, Inc., 1972, pp. 157-168.

Breman, Paul, ed. *You Better Believe It: The Penguin Book of Black Verse*. Baltimore: Penguin Books, Inc., 1973.

Brooks, Gwendolyn, ed. *A Broadside Treasury*. Detroit: Broadside Press, 1971, pp. 85-120.

Brown, Patricia L., Lee, Don L., and Ward, Francis, eds. *To Gwen with Love: An Anthology Dedicated to Gwendolyn Brooks*. Chicago: Johnson Pub. Co., 1971, pp. 68-69.

Chapman, Abraham, ed. *New Black Voices: An Anthology of Contemporary Afro-American Literature*. New York: New American Library, 1972, pp. 283-287.

Coombs, Orde, ed. *We Speak As Liberators: Young Black Poets*. New York: Apollo Editions, 1970, pp. 96-98.

Davis, Arthur P. and Redding, Saunders, eds. *Cavalcade: Negro American Writing from 1760 to the Present*. Boston: Houghton Mifflin Co., 1971, pp. 777-778.

Demarest, David P. and Lamdin, Lois S., eds. *The Ghetto Reader*. New York: Random House, Inc., 1970, p. 49; pp. 258-261.

Ford, Nick Aaron, ed. *Black Insights: Significant Literature by Afro-Americans—1760 to the Present*. Waltham, Mass.: Ginn & Co., 1971, pp. 358-360.

Giammanco, Roberto, ed. *Black Power. Potere Negro: Analisi e testimonianze*. Bari, Laterza, 1967, pp. 435-436.

Gross, Theodore L., ed. *A Nation of Nations: Ethnic Literature in America*. New York: The Free Press, 1971, p. 215.

Henderson, Stephen, ed. *Understanding the New Black Poetry: Black Speech and Black Music as Poetic References*. New York: William Morrow & Company, 1973, pp. 332-343.

Jordan, June, ed. *Soulscript: Afro-American Poetry.* New York: Doubleday and Company, 1970, pp. 92-94.

King, Woodie, ed. *Black Spirits: A Festival of New Black Poets in America.* New York: Random House, Inc., 1972, pp. 114-119.

Long, Richard A. and Collier, Eugenia, eds. *Afro-American Writing: An Anthology of Prose and Poetry.* 2 vols. New York Univ. Press, 1973.

Major, Clarence, ed. *The New Black Poetry.* New York: International Publishers Company, 1969, pp. 82-83.

Perkins, Eugene, ed. *Black Expressions: An Anthology of New Black Poets.* Chicago: Conda Printing, 1967.

Randall, Dudley, ed. *Black Poetry: A Supplement to Anthologies Which Exclude Black Poets.* Detroit: Broadside Press, 1969, pp. 41-45.

————. *The Black Poets.* New York: Bantam Books, Inc., 1971, pp. 295-309.

Randall, Dudley and Burroughs, Margaret G., eds. *For Malcolm: Poems on the Life and Death of Malcolm X.* Rev. (enlarged) ed. Detroit: Broadside Press, 1969, p. 64.

Robinson, William H., ed. *Nommo: An Anthology of Modern Black African and Black American Literature.* New York: Macmillan Publishing Co., 1972, pp. 446-452.

Turner, Darwin T., ed. *Black American Literature: Essays, Poetry, Fiction, Drama.* Columbus, Ohio: Charles E. Merrill Pub. Co., 1970, pp. 281-282.

Poems Published in Periodicals

Lee, Don L. "Assassination." *Negro Digest* XVII (Aug., 1968): 27.

————. "Back Again, Home." *Journal of Black Poetry* I (Summer, 1967): 24.

————. "The Black Christ." *Negro Digest* XVII (Sept.-Oct., 1968): 96-97.

————. "Blackman/an unfinished history." *Black World* XIX (May, 1970): 22-23.

———. "But He Was Cool." *The Campus Digest,* Tuskegee Institute, Ala., Sept. 22, 1972, p. 5.

———. "But He Was Cool." *Journal of Black Poetry* I (Spring, 1969): 12.

———. "Contradiction in Essence." *Journal of Black Poetry* I (Fall, 1967): 10.

———. "Don't Cry, Scream." *Journal of Black Poetry* I (Summer, 1968): 47-50.

———. "Don't Cry, Scream." *NOMMO: The Journal of the OBAC Writers' Workshop* I (Winter, 1969): 17-19.

———. "In the Interest of Black Salvation." *Negro Digest* XVI (June, 1967): 39.

———. "The Long Reality." *Freedomways* VII (Spring, 1967): 128.

———. "The Negro." *Negro Digest* XVII (Dec., 1967): 43.

———. "Nigerian Unity/or little niggers killing little niggers." *Negro Digest* XVIII (July, 1969): 18-21.

———. "One Sided Shoot-out." *Negro Digest* XIX (Jan., 1970): 90-91.

———. "Only a Few Left." *Negro Digest* XVI (Sept., 1967): 40.

———. "A Poem for Black Minds." *Journal of Black Poetry* I (Fall, 1967): 10.

———. "A Poem for Negro Intellectuals." *Journal of Black Poetry* I (Spring, 1969): 42.

———. "Positives: For Sterling Plumpp." *Freedomways* XI (Summer, 1971): 282-283.

———. "Remember to Remember the Un-Remembered." *Black World* XX (Sept., 1971): 68.

———. "Rise Vision Comin: May 27, 1972." *Black World* XXI (July, 1972): 26-28.

———. "To Be Quicker." *Black World* XIX (Sept., 1970): 86.

———. "We Go the Way of the New World." *Negro Digest* XVIII (Sept., 1969): 69.

Phonograph Records

Lee, Don L. *Gwendolyn Brooks Reading Her Poetry: With an Introductory Poem by Don L. Lee.* Caedmon TC 1244.
————. *Rappin' & Readin'.* Broadside Voices LP-BR-1.

Tapes

Broadside on Broadway: Seven Poets Read. Broadside Voices. Cassette. 1970.
Lee, Don L. *Don L. Lee Reads Don't Cry, Scream.* Broadside Voices. 5-inch reel. 3¾ i.p.s.
————. *Don L. Lee Reads We Walk the Way of the New World.* Broadside Voices. 5-inch reel. 3¾ i.p.s.

Video Tape

Lee, Don L. *Don L. Lee Reads at Martin Luther King High School.* 7/23/70. No. 37. Black and white. Rental. Community Learning Center; 85 W. Canfield; Detroit, Mich. 48201.

Miscellaneous

Anon. "Interview: The World of Don L. Lee." *The Black Collegian* I (Feb.-March, 1971): 24-27; 29; 33-34.
Lee, Don L. "The Bittersweet of Sweetback/ Or, Shake Yo Money Maker." *Black World* XXI (Nov., 1971): 43-48.
————. "A Reply from Don L. Lee." *Negro Digest* XVII (April, 1968): 96-98.

ABOUT DON L. LEE

Bibliographies

Fisher, Mary L., comp. *The Negro in America: A Bibliography.* 2nd (revised and enlarged) ed. Cambridge, Mass.: Harvard University Press, 1970.

Meserole, Harrison T., et al., comps. *1970 MLA International Bibliography* I. New York: MLA, 1972.

Turner, Darwin T. *Afro-American Writers.* Goldentree Bibliographies in Language and Literature. New York: Appleton-Century-Crofts, 1970.

Books

Brooks, Gwendolyn. *In the Mecca.* New York: Harper & Row Publishers, 1968.

————. *Report From Part One.* Detroit: Broadside Press, 1972.

Gibson, Donald B., ed. *Modern Black Poets: A Collection of Critical Essays.* Twentieth Century Views. Englewood Cliffs, N. J.: Prentice-Hall, Inc., 1973.

Kent, George E. *Blackness and the Adventure of Western Culture.* Chicago: Third World Press, 1972.

Plumpp, Sterling D. *Black Rituals.* Chicago: Third World Press, 1972.

Williams, Sherley Anne. *Give Birth to Brightness: A Thematic Study in Neo-Black Literature.* New York: Dial Press, Inc., 1973.

Articles

Anon. *"Black Spirits:* Book Party in Chicago." *Black World* XXII (Nov., 1972): 76-79.

Baker, Houston A., Jr. "The Fifties and Sixties." *Black Literature in America.* Ed. Houston A. Baker, Jr. New York: McGraw-Hill Book Co., 1971, pp. 303-309.

————. *"Utile, Dulce* and the Literature of Black America." *Black World* XXI (Sept., 1972): 30-35.

Barksdale, Richard K. "Humanistic Protest in Recent Black Poetry." *Modern Black Poets: A Collection of Critical Essays.* Ed. Donald B. Gibson. Twentieth Century Views. Englewood Cliffs, N. J.: Prentice-Hall, Inc., 1973, pp. 157-164.

Barksdale, Richard and Kinnamon, Keneth. "The Present Generation: Since 1945, Poetry." *Black Writers of America: A Comprehensive Anthology.* Eds. Richard Barksdale and Keneth

Kinnamon. New York: Macmillan Publishing Co., 1972, pp. 804-812.

Bell, Bernard W. "Contemporary Afro-American Poetry As Folk Art." *Black World* XXII (March, 1973): 16-26; 74-87.

————. "New Black Poetry: A Double-Edged Sword." *CLAJ* XV (Sept., 1971): 37-43.

Breman, Paul. "Poetry into the 'Sixties." *The Black American Writer, Volume II: Poetry and Drama.* Ed. C. W. Bigsby. Florida: Everett/Edwards, pp. 99-109.

Brooks, A. Russell. "The Motif of Dynamic Change in Black Revolutionary Poetry." *CLAJ* XV (Sept., 1971): 7-17.

Collier, Eugenia W. "Heritage From Harlem." *Black World* XX (Nov., 1970): 52-59.

Cunningham, James (Olumo). "Afro Blues." Introduction to *WATU: Journal of Black Poetry/Art,* IV (Cornell University, 1971), v-viii.

Davis, Arthur P. "The New Poetry of Black Hate." *CLAJ* XIII (June, 1970): 382-391.

Fuller, Hoyt W. "Algiers Journal." *Negro Digest* XVIII (Oct., 1969): 72-87.

————. "Chicago's OBAC: Portrait of Young Writers in a Workshop." *Negro Digest* XVII (Aug., 1968): 44-48; 79.

————. "The Game Gets Yeasty: On the Conference Front." *Negro Digest* XVII (July, 1968): 74-79.

————. "A 'Soul-In' at Fisk." *Negro Digest XVII* (July, 1968): 80.

Gayle, Addison, Jr. "The Politics of Revolution: Afro-American Literature." *Black World* XXI (June, 1972): 4-12.

Giddings, Paula. "From A Black Perspective: The Poetry of Don L. Lee." *Amistad 2.* Ed. John A. Williams and Charles F. Harris. New York: Random House, Inc., 1971, pp. 297-318.

Henderson, Stephen. "Introduction: The Forms of Things Unknown." *Understanding the New Black Poetry: Black Speech and Black Music as Poetic References.* Ed. Stephen Henderson. New York: William Morrow & Company, 1973, pp. 1-69.

————. " 'Survival Motion': A Study of the Black Writer and

the Black Revolution in America." In Cook, Mercer and Stephen E. Henderson. *The Militant Black Writer in Africa and the United States.* Madison: Univ. of Wisconsin Press, 1969, pp. 63-129.

LeGraham. "Black Poets at the Black Arts Convention, '67." *Journal of Black Poetry* I (Fall, 1967): 19-20.

Llorens, David. "Black Don Lee." *Ebony* XXIV (March, 1969): 72-78; 80.

Miller, Jeanne-Marie A. "A Black Poetry Festival in Washington, D.C." *Black World* XXI (Sept., 1972): 49-50.

Mphahlele, Ezekiel. "Voices in the Whirlwind: Poetry and Conflict in the Black World." *Voices in the Whirlwind and Other Essays.* New York: Hill and Wang, 1972, pp. 1-120. (Pp. 52-57 deal with Lee.)

Neal, Larry. "The Black Arts Movement." *The Black American Writer, Volume II: Poetry and Drama.* Ed. C. W. Bigsby. Florida: Everett/Edwards, 1969, pp. 187-202.

Palmer, R. Roderick. "The Poetry of Three Revolutionists: Don L. Lee, Sonia Sanchez, and Nikki Giovanni." *CLAJ* XV (Sept., 1971): 25-36.

Perkins, Eugene. "The Changing Status of Black Writers." *Black World* XIX (June, 1970): 18-23; 95-98.

Randall, Dudley. "An Answer to Don L. Lee's Review of Robert Hayden's *Kaleidoscope.*" *Negro Digest* XVII (April, 1968): 94-96.

————. "Broadside Press: A Personal Chronicle." *The Black Seventies.* Ed. Floyd B. Barbour. Boston: Sargent, Porter, Pub., 1970, pp. 139-148.

Robinson, William H., "Introduction." *Nommo: An Anthology of Modern Black African and Black American Literature.* Ed. William H. Robinson. New York: Macmillan Publishing Co., 1972, pp. 1-35.

Rodgers, Carolyn. "Black poetry—where it's at." *Negro Digest* XVIII (Sept., 1969): 7-16.

Serwaa, Amma. "How Don L. Lee Treats His Sisters." *Transition: Journal of the Department of Afro-American Studies* I, No. 2 (Howard University, 1972), 107-122.

Shands, Annette Oliver. "The Relevancy of Don L. Lee As A

Contemporary Black Poet." *Black World* XXI (June, 1972): 35-48.

Turner, Darwin T. Introduction (to "Poetry" section). *Black American Literature: Essays, Poetry, Fiction, Drama.* Ed. Darwin T. Turner. Columbus, Ohio: Charles E. Merrill Pub. Co., 1970, pp. 157-164.

————. "An Introduction: Afro-American Literary Critics." *Black World* XIX (July, 1970): 54-67.

Introductions to and Reviews of Lee's Books

Anon. "Book Review: *From Plan to Planet.*" *Black New Ark* II, March, 1973, 7.

Brooks, Gwendolyn. "A Further Pioneer." Introduction to Lee's *Don't Cry, Scream.* Detroit: Broadside Press, 1969, pp. 9-13.

Gant, Liz. "We Walk the Way of the New World; We A BaddDDD People; Half-Black, Half-Blacker." *Black World* XX (April, 1971): 84-87.

Gerald, Carolyn F. "Dynamite Voices I." *Black World* XXI (June, 1972): 52; 82-85.

Kaiser, Ernest. "Recent Books." *Freedomways* XIII (Winter, 1973): 90-91. (Review of Lee's *From Plan to Planet.*)

Knight, Etheridge. "Books Noted." *Negro Digest* XVII (June, 1968): 51-52. (Review of Lee's *Black Pride.*)

Randall, Dudley. Introduction to Lee's *Black Pride.* Detroit: Broadside Press, 1968, pp. 7-8.

Spady, James G. "*We Walk the Way of the New World:* A Book Review." *WATU: Journal of Black Poetry/Art* IV (Cornell University, 1971): 38-41.

Welburn, Ron. "Don't Cry, Scream!" *Negro Digest* XIX (Dec., 1969): 91-94.

Wilhite, Charlotte. "Dynamite Voices." *Black World* XXI (Dec., 1971): 52; 83-88.

Zahorski, Kenneth J. "Dynamite Voices: Black Poets of the 1960's." *CLAJ* XV (Dec., 1971): 257-259.

Tapes

Davis, Arthur P. *Don Lee and Other Revolutionary Poets.* A

radio talk in Professor Davis's Ebony Harvest Series. No. 25 of 26 lectures. Washington, D.C.: American University, 1973.

Miscellaneous

Alhamisi, Ahmed Akinwole. "News and History: Detroit." *Journal of Black Poetry* I (Special Pan-African Issue, 1970-1971): 99.

_____. "News: Detroit." *Journal of Black Poetry* I (Summer, 1968): 86; 87.

_____. "News: Detroit." *Journal of Black Poetry* I (Spring, 1969): 73; 74.

Anon. "Don L. Lee." *Journal of Black Poetry* I (Special Pan-African Issue, 1970-1971), inside front cover.

Anon. "Interview: Imamu Amiri Baraka." *The Black Collegian* III (March-April, 1973): 30-31; 33.

Bailey, Peter. "Nikki Giovanni: 'I Am Black, Female, Polite.'" *Ebony* XXVII (Feb., 1972): 48-50; 52; 54; 56.

Brooks, Gwendolyn. "Autobiographical Excerpt: *Report From Part One.*" *Black World* XXI (Sept., 1972): 4-12.

_____. "Don Lee." *Journal of Black Poetry* I (Fall, 1967): 23.

_____. "Introduction." *A Broadside Treasury.* Ed. Gwendolyn Brooks. Detroit: Broadside Press, 1971, p. 13.

_____. "Note." *Riot.* Detroit: Broadside Press, 1969, [p. 4].

_____. "A Report From: *Report From Part One.*" *Ebony* XXVIII (March, 1973): 116-120.

Fabio, Sarah Webster. "Books Noted." *Negro Digest* XVII (Sept.-Oct., 1968): 51-52.

Fuller, Hoyt W. "Books Received." *Black World* XX (Jan., 1971): 88.

_____. "Books Received." *Black World* XXI (Dec., 1971): 94.

_____. "Books Received." *Black World,* XXI (Feb., 1972), 94.

_____. "Cities in All Directions." *Negro Digest* XIX (Feb., 1970): 91.

_____. "Editor's Notes." *Negro Digest* XVI (June, 1967): 4.

————. "Independent Publications." *Negro Digest* XVII (May, 1968): 98.

————. "Miscellaneous Notes." *Black World* XIX (July, 1970): 68.

————. "Notes." *Negro Digest* XIX (Dec., 1969): 33.

————. "Paula Giddings." *Black World* XXI (Dec., 1971): 25.

————. "Perspectives." *Black World* XIX (Sept., 1970): 50.

————. "Perspectives." *Black World* XX (Dec., 1970): 66; 112; 113.

————. "Perspectives." *Black World* XX (Jan., 1971): 49.

————. "Perspectives." *Black World* XX (Feb., 1971): 49.

————. "Perspectives." *Black World* XX (March, 1971): 92.

————. "Perspectives." *Black World* XX (June, 1971): 50.

————. "Perspectives." *Black World* XX (Aug., 1971): 49-50.

————. "Perspectives." *Black World* XX (Sept., 1971): 80; 82-83.

————. "Perspectives." *Black World* XX (Oct., 1971): 50.

————. "Perspectives." *Black World* XXI (Dec., 1971): 80.

————. "Perspectives." *Black World* XXI (Aug., 1972): 49.

————. "Perspectives." *Black World* XXII (Nov., 1972): 50.

————. "Perspectives." *Black World* XXII (Jan., 1973): 90; 93.

————. "Perspectives." *Negro Digest* XVI (Sept., 1967): 50.

————. "Perspectives." *Negro Digest* XVII (Nov., 1967): 79-80.

————. "Perspectives." *Negro Digest* XVII (Dec., 1967): 91.

————. "Perspectives." *Negro Digest* XVII (Feb., 1968): 50.

————. "Perspectives." *Negro Digest* XVII (April, 1968): 49; 50; 82.

————. "Perspectives." *Negro Digest* XVII (May, 1968): 83.

————. "Perspectives." *Negro Digest* XVII (Aug., 1968): 49.

————. "Perspectives." *Negro Digest* XVIII (Jan., 1969): 81.

————. "Perspectives." *Negro Digest* XVIII (March, 1969): 86.

————. "Perspectives." *Negro Digest* XVIII (April, 1969): 73.

————. "Perspectives." *Negro Digest* XVIII (May, 1969): 90-91; 94.

————. "Perspectives." *Negro Digest* XVIII (June, 1969): 94.

————. "Perspectives." *Negro Digest* XVIII (July, 1969): 50.

————. "Perspectives." *Negro Digest* XVIII (Aug., 1969): 81.

————. "Perspectives." *Negro Digest* XVIII (Oct., 1969): 89.

————. "Perspectives." *Negro Digest* XIX (Jan., 1970): 83.

————. "Perspectives." *Negro Digest* XIX (March, 1970): 49.

————. "Perspectives." *Negro Digest* XIX (April, 1970): 79; 80; 81; 82.

Gayle, Addison, Jr. "Coming Home." *Black World* XXII (Jan., 1973): 52; 79-81.

Gerald, Carolyn F. "Afro-American Literature: An Introduction." *Black World* XXI (July, 1972): 51-52; 84.

————. "The Black Aesthetic." *Black World* XX (Oct., 1971): 51-52; 81-82.

————. "Black Arts." *Negro Digest* XIX (March, 1970): 92-93.

————. "Riot." *Black World* XIX (Aug., 1970): 51.

Giovanni, Nikki. "Black Poems, Poseurs and Power." *Negro Digest* XVIII (June, 1969): 30-34.

————. ["Curling"]. *Negro Digest* XVII (Aug., 1968): 86-88.

————. "Open Letter to Ron Welburn." *Negro Digest* XVIII (May, 1969): 97.

[Goncalves, Joe]. "Don L. Lee." *Journal of Black Poetry* I (Summer, 1967): 36.

————. "Don L. Lee." *Journal of Black Poetry* I (Fall, 1967): 37.

————. "Don L. Lee." *Journal of Black Poetry* I (Summer, 1968): 90.

Hudson, Jo. *"The Journey* and *The Black Hero." Black World* XX (March, 1971): 84-87.

————. "Well Organized Collection Examines Black Writers." *Freedomways* XIII (Winter, 1973): 77-79.

Jomo. "Ujamaa Festivals Featured Saturday and Sunday." *The Hilltop: Howard University Student Newspaper,* May 8, 1970, p. 9.

Jones, LeRoi and Neal, Larry. "Note to the First Paperback Edition of *Black Fire." Black Fire: An Anthology of Afro-American Writing.* Eds. LeRoi Jones and Larry Neal. New York:

William Morrow & Company, 1968, p. xvi.

Kent, George. "Shaping up the Field of Black Literature: Reviews of a Guide and a Bibliography." *Black World* XXI (Sept., 1972): 51-52; 87-89.

Ladner, Joyce A. *Tomorrow's Tomorrow: The Black Woman.* New York: Doubleday & Company, 1971 [p. v].

LeGraham. "Poetry and Related News from Motown. Detroit." *Journal of Black Poetry* I (Summer, 1967): 37-38.

Nicholas, A. Xavier. "A Conversation with Dudley Randall." *Black World* XXI (Dec., 1971): 26-34.

O'Daniel, Therman B. "CLA News." *CLAJ* XV (Dec., 1971): 261.

Parks, Carole A. "On Record." *Black World* XXI (March, 1972): 79.

Plumpp, Sterling D. "The Black Aesthetic." *Black World* XXI (June, 1972): 51.

Randall, Dudley. "How I Write." *Black World* XXI (May, 1972): 52.

————. "The Second Annual Black Arts Convention." *Negro Digest* XVII (Nov., 1967): 42-48.

Russell, Charlie L. "Black Spirits." *Black World* XXII (Jan., 1973): 86-87.

Shands, Annette Oliver. "Report From Part One: The Autobiography of Gwendolyn Brooks." *Black World* XXII (March, 1973): 70-71.

Spriggs, Ed. "News: Chicago." *Journal of Black Poetry* I (Winter, 1967-1968): 37.

————. "News: Chicago." *Journal of Black Poetry* I (Spring, 1969): 73.

————. "News: Detroit." *Journal of Black Poetry* I (Summer-Fall, 1969): 80.

Stephens, James M., Jr. "Anthology: Black Writers Workshop." *Black World* XX (June, 1971): 94-95.

Washington, Mary Helen. "Report From Part One: The Autobiography of Gwendolyn Brooks." *Black World* XXII (March, 1973): 51-52; 70.

————. "To Gwen—With Love." *Black World* XXI (Nov., 1971): 91-93.

Appendix
Reading List for "Worldview: Toward a New Consciousness"

(Spring semester, 1972-1973)   Don L. Lee, Instructor

I. OVERVIEW
   A. Chancellor Williams, *The Destruction of Black Civilization*
   B. Lao-tzu, *The Way of Life*
   Each of these texts will be frequent points of reference and should be studied immediately.

II. DEFINITION AND RE-DEFINITION (weeks one through three)
   A. Required Readings
      1. Johari M. Amini, *An Afrikan Frame of Reference*
      2. From Richard Wright, *White Man, Listen!*
         a. "The Psychological Reactions of Oppressed People" (Chap. 1)
      3. From Julius K. Nyerere, *Ujamaa: Essays on Socialism*
         a. "Education for Self-Reliance" (Chap. 4)
         b. "The Purpose Is Man" (Chap. 6)
      4. From Edward De Bono, *New Think: The Use of Lateral Thinking in the Generation of New Ideas*
         a. "Dominance" (Chap. 3)
      5. From *Nationalism in Asia and Africa,* ed. Elie Kedourie
         a. Edward W. Blyden, "The Negro in Ancient History"
         b. Cheikh Anta Diop, "The Contribution of Ethiopia-Nubia and of Egypt to Civilization"

137

6. Machiavelli, *The Prince*
7. *The Report from Iron Mountain,* ed. Leonard C. Lewin
8. Sterling D. Plumpp, *Black Rituals*
9. Samuel F. Yette, *The Choice: The Issue of Black Survival in America*

There will also be a lecture by an expert in this field.

B. Suggested Outside Reading
  1. Albert Memmi, *The Colonizer and the Colonized*
  2. Paulo Freire, *Pedagogy of the Oppressed*
  3. Don L. Lee, *From Plan to Planet*

III. CULTURE (weeks four through seven)
  A. Required Readings
    1. From Imamu Amiri Baraka, *Kawaida Studies: The New Nationalism*
      a. "Maulana Karenga & The Need for a Black Value System"
    2. Maulana Ron Karenga, "The Seven Criteria for Culture"
    3. From *The Black Aesthetic,* ed. Addison Gayle, Jr.
      a. Addison Gayle, Jr., "Introduction"
      b. Hoyt W. Fuller, "Towards a Black Aesthetic"
      c. Ron Karenga, "Black Cultural Nationalism"
      d. John O'Neal, "Black Arts: Notebook"
      e. Jimmy Stewart, "Introduction to Black Aesthetics in Music"
      f. J. A. Rogers, "Jazz at Home"
      g. LeRoi Jones, "The Changing Same (R&B and New Black Music)"
      h. Ortiz M. Walton, "A Comparative Analysis of the African and the Western Aesthetics"
      i. Langston Hughes, "The Negro Artist and the Racial Mountain"
      j. James A. Emanuel, "Blackness Can: A Quest for Aesthetics"
      k. W. Keorapetse Kgositsile, "Paths to the Future"
      l. Larry Neal, "The Black Arts Movement"

m. Ronald Milner, "Black Theater—Go Home"

n. Clayton Riley, "On Black Theater"

o. Richard Wright, "Introduction: Blueprint for Negro Writing"

p. Carolyn F. Gerald, "The Black Writer and His Role"

q. John Oliver Killens, "The Black Writer Vis-à-Vis His Country"

r. Ishmael Reed, "Can A Metronome Know The Thunder Or Summon A God?"

s. Addison Gayle, Jr., "The Function of Black Literature at the Present Time"

4. From Frantz Fanon, *The Wretched of the Earth*

a. "On National Culture"

Poetry, fiction, drama, and/or music will be supplied by instructor. There will also be a lecture by an expert in this field.

B. Suggested Outside Reading

1. Harold Cruse, *The Crisis of the Negro Intellectual*

2. E. Franklin Frazier, *Black Bourgeoisie*

3. Stephen Henderson, *Understanding the New Black Poetry*

4. Imamu Amiri Baraka, *Black Music*

IV. BIOLOGY, TECHNOLOGY, AND A LOOK INTO THE
. UN-THOUGHT-OF (weeks eight and nine)

A. Required Readings

1. Gordon R. Taylor, *The Biological Time Bomb*

2. From *The Technological Threat*, ed. Jack D. Douglas

a. Daniel Bell, "Notes on the Post-Industrial Society"

b. Norbert Wiener, "Some Moral and Technical Consequences of Automation"

3. From Erich Von Däniken, *Chariots of the Gods? Unsolved Mysteries of the Past*

a. "Are There Intelligent Beings in the Cosmos?"

4. Herbert M. Shelton, *Health for the Millions*

5. From Beni Casselle, "Back to Eatin'" (unpublished manuscript)

    a. "Water & Meat" (provided by instructor)

There will also be a lecture by an expert in this field.

B. Suggested Outside Reading

    1. Rachel Carson, *Silent Spring*

    2. Arnold Ehret, *A Scientific Method of Eating Your Way to Health: Arnold Ehret's Mucusless-Diet Healing System*

    3. Norman W. Walker, *Diet and Salad Suggestions for Use in Connection with Vegetable and Fruit Juices.*

V. THE WORLDRUNNERS: WHO ARE THEY AND HOW IS IT DONE? (weeks ten through twelve)

A. Required Readings

    1. Gabriel Kolko, *The Roots of American Foreign Policy*

    2. The Center for Black Education, *Afrikan Liberation*

    3. Shawna Maglangbayan, *Garvey, Lumumba, Malcolm: Black Nationalist-Separatists*

    4. Robert L. Allen, *Black Awakening in Capitalist America*

    5. Hoyt W. Fuller, *The Turning of the Wheel*

    6. Lerone Bennett, Jr., *Unity in the Black Community*

    7. From Harold Cruse, *The Crisis of the Negro Intellectual*

        a. "Jews and Negroes in the Communist Party"

    8. From Charles Wright Mills, *The Power Elite*

        a. "The Very Rich and the Higher Immorality"

    9. From *Nationalism in Asia and Africa*, ed. Elie Kedourie

        a. "Introduction" (pp. 1-152)

        b. Nicholas Ziadeh, "Arabism"

        c. Sun Yat-Sen, "The Principle of Nationalism"

        d. W. E. Burghardt Du Bois, "The Pan-African Movement"

        e. "The 'Circle'" (pp. 388-391)

        f. Josiah Mwangi Kariuki, "The 'Mau Mau' Oath"

        g. Frantz Fanon, "Concerning Violence"

There will also be a lecture by an expert in this field.

B. Suggested Outside Reading

1. Vincent Bakpetu Thompson, *Africa and Unity: The Evolution of Pan-Africanism*
2. Charles Wright Mills, *The Power Elite*
3. *History of the Pan-African Congress: Colonial and Coloured Unity, a Programme of Action,* ed. George Padmore
4. C[yril] L[ionel] R[obert] James, *A History of Pan-Afrikan Revolt*
5. Kwame Nkrumah, *Africa Must Unite*
6. Jerry S. Cohen and Morton Mintz, *America, Inc.: Who Owns and Operates the United States*

For further readings in all areas, see the "Functional Reading List," pp. 149-158 of *From Plan to Planet.*

Index

143